today and always
)but especially today(. II
xo. adrian michael

mirror you. check for blindspots.
inspire you. be your biggest fan.
better you. always seek to learn.
back you. support every endeavor.
heal you. water your wounds.
be you. choose yourself more.
love you. prioritize your heart.
trust you. deeply believe in you.
affirm you. memorize your language.
repeat you. every part of you.

xo. adrian michael

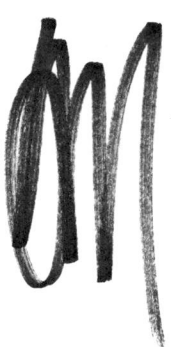

love language.

books by adrian michael

loamexpressions

blinking cursor

notes of a denver native son

blackmagic

lovehues

notes from a gentle man

blooming hearts

book of her book of she

for hearts that ache.

he was taught to be this way. I + II

giver. I + II + III

love language. I + II

love language. II

adrian michael

a lovasté project
in partnership with hwttbtw
published by
creative genius
CONCORDHAUS

lovaste.com

Copyright © 2021 by Adrian Michael Green

All rights reserved. No part of this book may be reproduced or transmitted in any form or by any means, electronic or mechanical, including photocopying, recording, or by any information storage and retrieval system, without written permission from the publisher.

Published by Creative Genius Publishing—
an imprint of lovasté

| Denver, CO | Concord, CA |

To contact the author:
    visit adrianmichaelgreen.com
To see more of the author's work:
    visit IG @adrianmichaelgreen
Book jacket designed by Adrian Michael Green

ISBN-13: 9798671577228

Printed in the United States of America

for lovers.
for those making waves.
for those trusting themselves.
for those journeying inward.

*a playlist**

right time x ye ali + reggie becton
waves x normani + 6lack
devotion x tone stith
like this x mitch + ann marie
still your best x giveon
overtime x bryson tiller
fire we make x alicia keys + maxwell
circles x trey songz
sweeter x leon bridges + terrace martin
floating x mannywellz + vanjess
make the most x lonr. + h.e.r.
the point of it all x anthony hamilton
find someone like you x snoh aalegra
self care x savannah cristina
superbloom x misterwives
naked x ella mai
the bones x maren morris
me x oshun
pick up your feelings x jazmine sullivan
home x joseph solomon
resting x joseph august
someone to love x jon b.
deep end x xavier omar + sango
the beginning x alina baraz
good love x 11:11
beautiful x mali music

incense. palo santo. candles. sage.
tea. whiskey. wine. water. beer.

to be listened to. lit and sipped while reading or between readings for ultimate experience.

words for you

let go of what you are holding onto.	1
four types of love you deserve.	2
when to love more. II.	3
four wants every soul aches for.	4
ten reminders to breathe in.	5
five things to be grateful for.	6
four myths about therapy.	7
the ten re-commitments.	8
when you thrust yourself all-in.	9
four easy things to notice.	10
worthmore.	11
feeling is a love language.	12
make sure to prioritize you.	13
eleven soul duties to watch out for.	14
what you didn't know you needed to hear. II.	15
the most beautiful i am into you.	16
when someone who loves you asks.	17
four relationships to never force.	18
ten signs it is time for change.	19
twenty beautiful things to tell yourself.	20
four requests for august.	21
you deserve the best love.	22
vibe protection.	23
asking for help is a love language.	24
requirements.	25
thirteen beliefs that you have to believe.	26
fourteen stay's to bloom into something beautiful.	27
don't be the thief of your own joy.	28
your love is. an ode to you beautiful giver.	29
four registers that make a difference.	30
four did you know's to wake up to.	31

words for you

six sometimes to examine deeply.	32
33 lessons.	33
four irrefutable facts about you.	34
when you look in the mirror recite these words.	35
you shouldn't have to.	36
what we all need.	37
three types of safety you deserve.	38
the most beautiful goodbye.	39
humans bloom because of you.	40
the four best investments.	41
ten quiet whispers to always say out loud.	42
the stars dance for you.	43
what to do when stuff doesn't go your way.	44
sharing music is a love language.	45
as soon as you get this.	46
fifteen you don't have to's just for you.	47
be prepared.	48
twelve signs you're in a toxic relationship.	49
three reasons you are really angry.	50
effort is a love language.	51
goodness grows towards you.	52
the world feels you no matter what you do.	53
routine.	54
emotional labor is cancelled.	55
ten all right's that make you human.	56
take this with you.	57
the sky is whatever color you want it to be.	58
two reminders.	59
full stop.	60
you are an old soul.	61
ten keys to a meaningful life.	62

words for you

one part of your story.	63
keep their name on your lips.	64
your greatest affirmation.	65
let them.	66
two secrets from the universe to practice.	67
considerate.	68
love on some you.	69
everevolving love.	70
can't be loved seperately.	71
stay close to hearts that care like yours.	72
for things to grow water must fall.	73
cry into the wind.	74
four parts of you to always protect.	75
purpose.	76
five post-it notes to place on your wall of healing.	77
four gems to remember when feeling unsteady.	78
a letter to you.	79
five seconds of advice.	80
sometimes flowers don't want you to be gentle.	81
five when's to remember.	82
the most beautiful good morning.	83
center you more.	84
double double standard.	85
five answers to questions you never ask.	86
self-awareness is a love language.	87
you deserve this kind of love. II.	88
trust is a love language.	89
four things you are entitled to do. II.	90
twelve roses to give yourself more often.	91
ten small and big things.	92
five things you can't mess up.	93

words for you

remember.	94
don't overthink. overfeel.	95
i hope today deserves you.	96
don't lose yourself chasing after others.	97
no longer accepting. III.	98
fourteen carries to wear in sunlight.	99
when you know you have learned and grown.	100
starting point.	101
you already know this.	102
you already know this. II.	103
the only one in your way is you.	104
the most beautiful goodnight.	105
every breath is a chance to heal.	106
arrest the killers of breonna taylor.	107
five do not oaths to chant.	108
more time.	109
eight mistakes you need to forgive yourself for.	110
let's talk is a love language.	111
two notes about growth.	112
the you you need to know more of.	113
don't fake full when feeling empty.	114
to better appreciate yourself.	115
when taken for granted.	116
what may never come.	117
fifteen deep breaths to let in.	118
two truths about pain.	119
you deserve this.	120
four truths that have always been true.	121
twelve songs written in the key of you.	122
three reminders to ease your mind.	123
five signs you're going in circles.	124

words for you

re-introduce yourself.	125
five ways to say no without saying no.	126
rest is a love language.	127
when you want something real.	128
what love isn't.	129
we need each other.	130
twelve positive assumptions.	131
patience is a love language.	132
love is a language understood without words.	133
a beautiful libation to pour for yourself.	134
enough is a love language.	135
an anti-racist statement.	136
definitions of privilege that are sadly unknown.	137
five types of rest you deserve.	138
you already know this. III.	139
flags that let you know who people really are.	140
it's okay. IV.	141
what you need to hear but haven't told yourself yet.	142
six strengths.	143
four signs you still have more healing to do.	144
ten necessities to pick up.	145
return to love.	146
four masks to stop wearing.	147
8 lessons.	148
ten apologies you don't need to give.	149
four be's to remind you to be gentle with yourself.	150
something beautiful you haven't felt.	151
losing is a beautiful happening.	152
fall. fall. fall.	153
choose yourself.	154
trust yourself.	155

let go of what you are holding onto.

take a deep breath. let the day or yesterday or the thought of tomorrow go. any stress release it. tell it to leave you alone. you deserve some peace while those that cause the distress get to go on and lose no sense of normalcy. take hold of your pieces others have no business having. don't lose sleep over people who aren't losing theirs. reclaim the trust in you and trust in you. remember that heart in you. full of power and wonder. believe in you. all of you. let go of what you are holding onto. and rinse into the next venture. the next what will be feeling lighter and with your own blessing. your own verification. your own validation. your own accreditation. for anything outside of you comes with its own restrictions. its own expectations. its own pressures that contort you into what you no longer want anything to do with. no longer want any energy from. no longer recognize. and what is ahead is supposed to feel new. even if it feels more of the same. just with new eyes. to see you better. to determine what parts of you must now take lead. must be re-oriented and polished. the thing about letting go of what you are holding onto is that it involves a cleansing practice. a taking of inventory. a putting up the mirror. a putting down the ego. a closing ritual to open to open to open what couldn't take on air under the old conditions. and only you only you only you know how to breathe newly. you've been holding old breath in and now it is time to exhale. and unleash what leashed you. held you. locked you. blocked you. and make room for beautiful possibility. beautiful searching. beautiful love. that will ultimately catapult you where you couldn't get to before. not because you weren't ready)you've always been ready(but because the low hum of your calling couldn't cut through all the noise to be heard effectively. now you can hear it. the pulsing. the pulling. the pounding. that won't go away. answer. leap. believe. this is your beginning. your awakening. your time. xo.

love language.

four types of love you deserve.

healthy love. complete. supportive. nourishing.
consistent love. steady. compatible. aligned.
patient love. stays. empathetic. accepting.
full love. deep. harmonious. kind.

you deserve to see and feel and be wrapped up
in thoughtful long lasting relationships that water
and sun and appreciates you. anything less than magic
is too shallow and not worthy of your energy.
protect your heart and remain beautifully you.

***

a new day a new beginning a new chance. you get to be a better human. work on something that fills you and helps someone directly or indirectly. since we all deserve love then we all must foster and practice it. keep up the work you are doing but don't give up because it's getting to be too uncomfortable or too hard. stay there. that is where the real learning happens. that's how pure gold is made. by standing in the fire. be the one that stays even if those around you can't take the heat. become the fire that never goes out. this is the only way true love and change comes about. become the smoke that is seen from far away to alarm to warn to remind what good love consists of. and if they can't see it)they can see it(they are choosing what you can't choose for them. just be careful not to be your own detriment waiting weighting wading in the ashes of the uncaring. in the unloving. in the unkind. take your advice and find yourself running towards real love and not stranded in trash love.

when to love more. II

in the now.
in the heat.
in the thick.
in the sore.
in the chaos.
in the don't.
in the down.
in the fall.
in the crash.
in the flames.

***

you are a stayer. you stay. you last. you fight. you give your all even when your all takes up the slack of others when it shouldn't at all. but in the gap of that slack is a too much. too much lee-way. too much hope things will change. too much giving the thousandth chance. but that too much doesn't mean anything other than it tells you the character you have. the character you are. the humanity so entrenched in you. it gives more than enough and can be taken for granted but don't you wall up and become them. don't you stop that heart of yours. let no one ever say you didn't try. sometimes staying means leaving.

so love more by loving yourself more. leave more room for you. so you can look at you and say you did the best you could for as long as you could and must do what you must do or it will crush you when you have been crushed enough)too much(and now loving more means digging deeper or getting the fuck out of the hole you've been digging alone.

four wants every soul aches for.

respect. to be admired. valued. reassured.
belonging. to be part of. received. welcomed.
devotion. to be loved. wanted. appreciated.
attention. to be seen. understood. heard.

seek out relationships that don't take advantage of all you have to offer. stay with those who care deeply and want you to thrive instead of keeping you down. be the reason someone smiles and feels truly wonderful like no one else ever could.

***

you are the home everyone wants to shelter in. the heart that keeps secrets safe. the lover that knows how to read energy. you are what every soul aches for. and you're far too humble to know it.

i hope there was some moment in this day that made you smile. that the tension in your body dropped out of you even if momentarily to feel some relief. i hope you heard your heart beat and listened to it say thank you. i hope you were told how much someone loves you. if no one told you they love you know that i do. i do. i hope you thought of someone other than yourself today. stood up and spoke truth to someone who needed to hear about themselves. i hope you listened when you wanted to just interrupt. i hope you learned one new thing in how to be a better human. i hope you get good rest when you can. the world needs you but you also need you. take care of yourself. take care of yourself.

ten reminders to breathe in.

you are loved.
you are worthy.
you are sacred.
you are enough.
you are breathtaking.
you are unique.
you are deserving.
you are capable.
you are divine.
you are beautiful.

never let anyone try to make you feel anything
other than incredible. you are all these things and
more. and more. and more. so much more. you
are the light of all lights. and don't even know it.

***

you don't understand the magnitude of you. the deep deep of you.
the words that don't exist to describe you. you are out of this world
and of something more magic. more boundless.
your gravity is pure bliss.

five things to be grateful for.

for life.
for beauty.
for love.
for joy.
for you.

set intentions today to be present with yourself. to experience your fullness. your oneness. your every ness. turn into you. feel you and remind remind remind that you are. and that is always enough.

***

you are. and that is always enough.
you are. and that is always enough.
you are. and that is always enough.
you are. and that is always enough.
you are. and that is always enough.
you are. and that is always enough.
you are. and that is always enough.
you are. and that is always enough.
you are. and that is always enough.
you are. and that is always enough.
you are. and that is always enough.
you are. and that is always enough.
you are. and that is always enough.

don't forget to be grateful for you. all of you.
the where of you. the heart of you. the how of you.
the why of you. the beauty of you.

four myths about therapy.

reserved only for the wealthy.
reserved only for white people.
reserved only for those in crisis.
reserved only for the weak.

let go of the idea that you can't access or show up
or prioritize your wellness. asking for help before
matters get worse or taking preventative measures
is a whole love language. a full message to self
that says: you matter. you're worthy. you're loved.

don't apologize for being your full experience. your full light. your full nature. being yourself allows you to heal yourself. and healing is your best feature. there are stigmas to therapy that must be debunked and let go of. too many hold on to the idea that it is only reserved for some. i admit i have avoided formal therapy for a list of reasons but we do know the practice itself has human error and people who do not have the cultural competency or cultural fluency or cultural understanding of those with different experiences tend to revert to what they have been taught and lean into their own bias and too often do more harm. there are many forms of therapy. your person cannot be your therapy session. your person can't be your rehab center your dumping ground your punching bag. talk to someone. find a therapist. discuss what is holding you hostage. free yourself. free yourself. free yourself. unpack the toxins you are keeping in your body. i am in therapy and it is transformative. i have to do my own work. you have to do your work. we have to heal ourselves and be better for one another. there is nothing weak about centering your wellness. it is one of the strongest things you could ever do.

the ten re-commitments.

re-commit to love yourself during hard moments.
re-commit to breathe deep when you just want to run.
re-commit to clap for yourself when others do not.
re-commit to accept the parts of you seen and unseen.
re-commit to own your mistakes.
re-commit to take responsibility for your actions.
re-commit to choose you more often.
re-commit to open your heart and let others in.
re-commit to think and grow rich holistically.
re-commit to do your work and be a good person.

commiting to you is a daily endeavor. a daily practice. a daily breath. a daily meditation. it is an unresolving reminder to put you in front of you and mirror what has been stone wall. to mirror what was unseen and to always always always re-commit so not to ever forget what it is that keeps you going. this may sound redundant or unimportant or something you've heard as cliché but you are not a cliché or someone to be taken lightly anymore. you are everything and everything about you must be forefront and breathed in deeply. smoothly. intentionally. confidently. always. always. always. always. so re-commit and re-solve and re-mind and re-heart you. and do it all again the next day and the next.

***

what a commitment you are. the best kind. not the kind you feel tied down to. the kind that fills you to the brim overflowing with joy. the kind that nothing else no one else is worth savoring but you.

when you thrust yourself all-in.

when you thrust yourself all-in
   all-in in a relationship.
   all-in in a job.
   all-in on a project.
   all-in on a dream.
   all-in on an unknown.

you practically are saying
no matter what happens
you gave everything
and leave nothing
to chance. people
who do this truly
are the greatest
dreamers and lovers
and friends and even
if it doesn't work out
they hold their hearts high.

your all-in love is the greatest love.
even your mediocre surpasses anything
anyone could dream of.

***

give your all all. not some. not kind of. not low. all. stop half doing anything because anything less than all is empty. anything less than you is tragic. your best is always a beautiful everything.

***four easy things to notice
and critique in others.***

wrongdoing.
flaws.
imperfection.
mistakes.

the challenge is

to notice those in ourselves.
to not judge others outloud.
to examine own faults.
to give others grace.
to understand that not everyone
will do what you do how you do it.
let them be them. you be you.
everyone is doing the best they can.

***

easy to pinpoint flaws in others)or the perception of flaws(and pass judgement and talk mess about what you would do differently. it is projection and dismissive and passing on what is assumed to be helpful but in turn is harmful. everyone is on their own path. if they ask for advice give it. but do not for one second think you are the holder of all things and expert in life. everyone is doing the best they can. reconsider what you would tell someone else and tell it to yourself or keep it to yourself. before sharing anything consider the root of your response and wonder where it is coming from. if it is crucial or inconsiderate. selfish or in partnership. loving or spiteful. the most terrible offering is unsolicited advice.

worthmore.

you are not worthless you are worthmore. always remember that the next time someone)including you(tries to convince you otherwise.

feeling is a love language.
it says:

feel me. notice me. emote me. breathe me in.
so much is going on that it's easy to forget me.
easy to avoid me. easy to leave me. easy to
abandon me. easy to rain check me. easy to
lose me. but that swelling in me is a swelling
in you. and you can't keep running from your
shadow. mirrors have a way of reflecting even
if you can't look directly at yourself. so dig.
and dig. and dig. and dig. deeper. when you
think you have struck gold there is more.
find me. hold me. polish me. honor me.
connect me back to you. without me
there is no you. no love. no light.
express me. fear nothing here.

***

when you are that person. when you have that person that says fear nothing here. be everything here. every every of you is welcome here. duplicate that. relish that. stay as long as you can. notice the monuments that are built in your honor just because you are free to be yourself. share yourself. exist yourself. imagine all the people barriered and barred and outcast because of what people say and feel and do and may not even know it. be who you are and if they can't handle you leave them vacant and house yourself elsewhere.

make sure to prioritize you.

make sure to prioritize you.
make sure to prioritize you.
make sure to prioritize you.
make sure to prioritize you.
make sure to prioritize you.
make sure to prioritize you.
make sure to prioritize you.
make sure to prioritize you.
make sure to prioritize you.
make sure to prioritize you.
make sure to prioritize you.
make sure to prioritize you.
make sure to prioritize you.
make sure to prioritize you.
make sure to prioritize you.
make sure to prioritize you.
make sure to prioritize you.
make sure to prioritize you.
make sure to prioritize you.
make sure to prioritize you.
make sure to prioritize you.
make sure to prioritize you.
make sure to prioritize you.
make sure to prioritize you.
make sure to prioritize you.

***

keep choosing you even when choosing you is misunderstood. keep prioritizing you when prioritizing you is challenging. keep you at the top when others forget. you can't forget you. you can't.

eleven soul duties to watch out for.

watch out for other people.
watch out for how you treat people.
watch out for how you make people feel.
watch out for the stories you tell yourself.
watch out for what you bring from your past.
watch out for the inner child in you.
watch out for your dreams to come true.
watch out for people who just take.
watch out for all beings with great care.
watch out for your mental health.
watch out for that big beautiful heart.

you can't control what others think feel or do but you can.
be on alert and notice how you show up. how you treat.
how you consider. how you love. be good to yourself and others.

***

make that decision to lean in even if it is too difficult. even a step towards is closer than you already are. nothing will change or get done unless you face it. unless you do something. it doesn't have to be big. it doesn't have to be solved. it doesn't have to be done all in one day. it does have to take effort. it does have to be your choice. it does have to be meaningful. whatever that means to you. tie it to a reason. your reason. so you can then anchor back to it when the lean in becomes unbearable. when the lean in gets too hot. when the choice to face feels insurmountable. remembering the why will soften the temperature as you become the fire you need.

what you didn't know you needed to hear. II

you are healing and don't even know it.
you are going through a growth spurt.
you are deserving of better everything.
you are not a convenience store.
you are making a big difference.
you are incredible but sometimes forget.
you are a rare find still looking for yourself.
you are wandering but far far from lost.
you are true to yourself so stay that way.
you are at a breaking point but will not break.
you are amazing and don't need to prove it.
you are a wild heart too magic to tame.

***

you are a wild heart too magic to tame. too enough for some. too many everything's to outline. you are a work of art and haven't begun your master masterpiece. a beautiful curious soul in search of more.

choose good good deep deep profound rest this weekend. don't rationalize or try to convince or explain your choice of play. rest in whatever that looks like and stay there til your mind stops telling you stop choosing rest. and then keep resting. and keep resting. and keep resting. and when you're ready choose rest some more. you deserve a break. do this more often with intention. notice how you feel when you do this. how you approach each interaction each person each relationship. when it breaks down you will know why.

the most beautiful i am into you
without saying i am into you.

i have loved you for a thousand lifetimes.
still it feels like we just met. our souls mixed
and i've been a goner since always. i never
want to be away from you. i just called
to hear your heartbeat over the phone. i made
this playlist for our car ride. is it wrong of me
to want this moment not to end so as you
leave i'm texting you to begin our next past
midnight conversation. do you already have
plans for your forever or can we spend it
together. i have loved you long before i had
the courage to tell you. you complete me.

it's impossible to be away from you too long. one second is too far away from you. one exhale is one kiss too far away from you. one heartbeat is too lonely if not by you. it's hard because loving you is deep breath itself. deep. deep. breath.

***

hearing your voice for the first time is a sound no one could ever forget. it matches your smile. matches your dimples. matches your confidence. matches your beauty. your voice is the kind of voice that stops and starts hearts. you stop and start hearts. what a present you are. what a presence you are. being into you is something hard to quantify and put into any clear explanation. like experiencing an out of body experience and having to re-tell a dream you didn't know you were in. you just feel it. you feel you. the best kind of filling.

when someone who loves you asks

where are you.
when are you coming home.
when will i see you again.
are you on your way.

they are really saying

i miss you.
i can't wait much longer.
you are too far away.
be with me.

hold onto those who hear your call for
loving closeness. this isn't needy. this is
your love language requesting quality time.

***

you are someone's favorite song. favorite melody. favorite chorus. favorite beat. favorite verse. your falsetto is their downfall their rising heartbeat their favorite part on repeat. you are a classic timeless feeling wrapped in beautiful noise.

people look to you and you don't even realize it. that's another reason you are so beloved. you don't let your glow overshadow your down to earth nature. what a humble lover you are. what a humble lover you are. it is as if all the rare traits collided when you came into existence as proclamation as divine intervention as innerwordly blessing to grace life. to grace light. to grace love.

four relationships to never force.

love.
healing.
friendship.
advice.

it takes time to develop. to nurture. to get to.
pushing only furthers away. pulling gives no choice. so just be. let. let. let. and what flows is meant to be even if it's not how you had it look and sound and feel in your mind. too much force creates too much pressure and what could have been becomes a never will. patience makes everything grow fonder.

you are what makes everything grow fonder.

***

don't rush. don't force. don't push. don't pry. don't short cut. don't avoid. don't run around. check back in and see how you feel when you just let. when you just be. flow is a game changer. if you are willing to try a different approach.

ten signs it is time for change.
for something new. for you
to re-consider what is best
for your heart. and decide.
and be rooted. content.
in your decision. to move on.

your heart isn't in it.
your mind is distracted.
your intuition is gasping for air.
your desire has shifted.
your soul is fed up.
your light has outgrown the shade.
your feelings aren't reciprocated.
your love is in need of water.
your creativity is being held back.
your next self is waiting for you.

you should go wherever you need to grow. to expand. to feel. to be seen. to belong. if it isn't where you already are it might be time to listen to your heart.

***

your intuition knows you know. knows you can heart it. feel it. but too often you go the other direction. make the different call. this time. next time. tune into what your conscious is telling you and trust it. trust you. don't make decisions off of what others think anymore. make decisions off of what you know needs to be done. and be okay with what comes after. you are ready for the after. it's just that you are holding onto the now and fearful for what you don't know. that's normal. now let go and root into your power. root into your power.

twenty beautiful things to tell yourself.

come close for a minute. rest rest rest your weight
down for a moment. look at everything you have
gone through. look. back then you couldn't see
the light but you've always been the light. and
see how far you have carried yourself. it has been
a journey. hard. you've scraped and fumbled. ran
away. ran towards. but you stayed. you stayed.
be proud. hella proud. be emotional. a ways still
to go. but i need you to know something no one will say this way:
you are the only one that knows what it's like to be you and i see
you all of you the heart of you and you do you so elegantly.
thank you. the lover in me honors the lover in you.

***

look how far you've come. this is no easy feat. seriously. all this hardship. the discomfort. the aches. the unknowing. the wondering. but you haven't backed down even if you have had moments with your back trembling. be proud of yourself. toast yourself. cheers yourself. you deserve to be grateful for you. i am. i am. i am.

four requests for august.

be gentle.
be grounding.
be ocean.
be restorative.

may this new month be a new chapter. new
season. new balance. new breath. take it on
with fervor and zeal and give permission to
discover more of you. unpeel and lay out.
direct yourself to yourself and let go of
whatever needs to be let go of. let in
all that will grow you beautifully.

you. all of you. every line of you. is so beautifully designed. so elegantly made. if they can't see the divine in you don't waste a moment to convince them of your oasis. eventually)always eventually(they will crawl to your ocean and request replenishment.

***

time is going by and a new moon is upon us. a new cycle. a new timeline. a new opportunity. to begin again. to renew. to start up. to check in. to refresh. take a chance you didn't take yesterday or last week or last month or last year. push yourself closer to yourself and be in awe of what you've been missing all this time. perhaps august will be good to us. perhaps august isn't ready for all the abundance everyone is about to experience. or perhaps august knows this is the season of you and has been preparing for your harvest. take the time to figure it out. peace be your august.

you deserve the best love.

you deserve the best love.
the kind that meets you. exceeds you.
hears you. sees you. reaches you. touches you.
caresses you. validates you. inspires you.
admires you. surprises you.
completes you. supports you. stretches you.
because the best love deserves the best love back.
because the best love deserves the best love back.
because the best love deserves the best love back.
because the best love deserves the best love back.
because the best love deserves the best love back.

***

whatever best love means to you make sure you get it don't settle or ignore or give up or lower. get what you need or live a life unfulfilled. and if anyone makes you doubt makes you fear makes you lapse makes you feel as if what you are chasing isn't real or for you or worth the reach tell them to direct their words somewhere else. your heart is made up. your heart is made up. your heart is made up of possibility. made up of magic. made up of stuff too many people throw out because they were made to believe that inner love inner divine inner course inner work inner pursuit inner paving was worthless and to focus on outward appeals outward conditions to get you running for others instead of running for what motivates you. so go and do what inspires you. so go and do what stretches you. so go and do what supports you. so go and do what touches you. so go and do what exceeds you. so go and do what hears you. so go and do what sees you. so go and do what caresses you. so go and do what validates you. go and do. and keep going. keep doing.

five ways to prevent others
from messing with your vibe.

take a breath. pause and collect yourself.
notice. the impact their presence has on your body.
choose. if you want to respond or not.
say thank you. to any and all unsolicited advice.
re-focus. tend to what's most important.

distractions are meant to send you on a detour away from yourself. they come in the form of people and substances.
your good energy is yours.
don't apologize for protecting you and your peace.

you are a vibe. a peace. a declaration.
an entire galaxy covered in beautiful skin.

***

access to you is a privilege. always has been. always will be. just because someone makes a request doesn't mean you have to take it. this doesn't mean you are shut off. it means you are bound by the laws you have agreed to with your own body mind spirit. your peace is yours and anyone who can't honor that are the very ones set to shatter what they come across and that is what you don't have time for. your good energy is nectar so many want to taste but will never be granted access if they keep trying to take you away from you. and you are never one to force access to other people which is such a massive difference. such a thoughtful way of interacting because you know what invasion feels like. you know what the invade and the force and the clenching does to a person. but others think they have a right to anything they see. and their approach has such toxicity. maintain your boundaries. maintain your vibe.

asking for help is a love language.
it says:

there is a need in me that i've tried to fill. tried to
solve on my own and i am reaching out to you as
someone i trust to support me. this isn't easy for
me as i normally do things and figure out and fix
and struggle alone. if this is any burden to you
i'll take the ask back but there is no capacity
anymore. no air difficult to breathe lungs
feel tight in my chest just listen. just
hear my vulnerability without one
word one criticism one sigh. and
be there. show up. i'm strong.
i don't have all the answers.

***

you are strong enough and wise enough and brave enough and vulnerable enough to know that you do not have all the answers. takes courage to let someone in but asking for help gives you more room in your body to breathe. and you deserve to not keep doing all that you are doing by yourself. you deserve to not keep doing all that you are doing by yourself. you deserve to not keep doing all that you are doing by yourself. relief is on its way to you the moment you hold asking for help in your mind and it gets to you quicker when you verbalize it follow it share it manifest it lift it away from your chest for another to beautifully breathe in as for so long they were looking for some way some how some chance to carry some of you. not because you aren't strong)you are strong(but because you deserve more room to do what you haven't been able to do. make room for you. give yourself persmission to ask for help.

requirements.

don't apologize for exiting toxic wastelands.
your mental space requires this of you.

thirteen beliefs that you have to believe.

believe you are worthy.
believe you are enough.
believe you are a shining star.
believe you are ready.
believe you inspire others just by being you.
believe you when no one believes in you.
believe your heart is healing you can't see it.
believe you and your love to be intoxicating.
believe you are beautiful even if no one says it.
believe your purpose is changing lives.
believe you can do what you put your mind to.
believe you make this place a better place.
believe.you are everything you need you need.

***

believe. you are everything you need you need. breathe some you in and gather and gather and gather all the you you've forgotten about.

another day another better version of you to create. to appreciate. to recognize. to validate. to see. to let be. let breathe. yesterday can't define you. today is your chance to be who you weren't the day before. the future is being watered when you breathe yourself in. when you believe in yourself. when you be and leave all that nonsense that tries to stop you. you'll know where you are meant to be as soon as you start to remember who you are. when what surrounds you feels familiar. like you have been there before. like what is there has been waiting for you to come home. back to you. the power of you is the belief in you. and when you do that. no stopping you. unstoppable you is the most beautiful version of you.

fourteen stay's to bloom into something beautiful.

stay soft.
stay vigilant.
stay above.
stay alert.
stay radiant.
stay engaged.
stay fly.
stay steady.
stay consistent.
stay determined.
stay water.
stay fire.
stay you.
stay. grow into the you you've been waiting to
arrive. and become. fall back in love with you.

***

keep keeping on. fight. determine. twist. shake. don't settle. never settle. battle and do not let up. too much is at stake. you are at stake. resorting to old ways will get you further away from where you need to be. where we need to be. stay. stay. stay. don't turn away. you cannot look away. face this. face you. show up and show how this is done. no need to pretend you got it all together. it's not about that. it's about the warrior in you and the lover in you and the sovereign in you and the magician in you to see themselves. their full self. in you. it's always been you. never let anyone force you to believe you deserve scraps when you deserve everything everything.

don't be the thief of your own joy.

don't be the thief of your own joy.
don't be the thief of your own joy.
don't be the thief of your own joy.
don't be the thief of your own joy.
don't be the thief of your own joy.
don't be the thief of your own joy.
don't be the thief of your own joy.
don't be the thief of your own joy.
don't be the thief of your own joy.
don't be the thief of your own joy.
don't be the thief of your own joy.
don't be the thief of your own joy.
don't be the thief of your own joy.
don't be the thief of your own joy.
don't be the thief of your own joy.
don't be the thief of your own joy.
don't be the thief of your own joy.
don't be the thief of your own joy.
don't be the thief of your own joy.
don't be the thief of your own joy.
don't be the thief of your own joy.
don't be the thief of your own joy.
don't be the thief of your own joy.
don't be the thief of your own joy.
don't be the thief of your own joy.
don't be the thief of your own joy.
don't be the thief of your own joy.
don't be the thief of your own joy.
don't be the thief of your own joy.
don't be the thief of your own joy.
don't be the thief of your own joy.
don't be the thief of your own joy.

your love is. an ode to you beautiful giver.

your love is butterfly kisses on summer evenings.
your love is soul stirring heart beats throbs sighs.
your love is deep belly breaths laughs howls.
your love is *i'd do anything for you love. anything.*
your love is walking up honey hills bright-eyed.
your love is magic firestorms amidst chaos.
your love is *for better and for worse.*
your love is safe and healing wonderful wonderfull.
your love is sensitive and special. whole. home.
your love is everything beautiful and breathtaking.
your love is *through all the ups and downs.*

***

your love is life-changing. heart quenching. roots neverending. remember you are everything beautiful and breathtaking. sometimes you forget this. don't forget this. breathe this. be this. hold this. love this. love you. love you. because any ode dedicated to you is laced with truth. always truth. heartfelt and lovefelt and soulfelt and allfelt with sincerity because that is what is required. that is what is coming to you. always coming to you. even if it doesn't show up how you need it to show up. everything is all right when you touch. when you breathe. when you you. and when you you everything falls into place. everything is as it should be. because your love is. and anything that is is enough. is necessary. is outstanding. is instanding. filling and satiable. you can't be re-created but you deserve to be loved as is. with no expectation to change how great you are. how great you are. how. great. you. are. stay beautiful lover. stay beautiful dear giver. stay you. stay you.

four registers that make a difference.

register to vote. elect and choose fairness.
register to talk. communicate your opinions.
register to give. share what you have and know.
register to love. commit with your whole being.

show up. sign up. practice what you know to be
good and true and thoughtful and respectful and
think about your impact on others. think about
your ripple effect. think about how important
and vital your advocacy is. your voice matters.

people turn to you for a reason. use your influence for greater good.

***

what is life if not for its challenges. if not for its adventures. if not for its opportunities. if not for its space to figure out whys and hows and whens and whats to open and wonder and figure but but but we make it hard)too unfortunately hard(for everyone to have this space. for everyone to have liberty. it isn't reasonable to seek equality but seeking fairness is the mission)shouldn't be the mission should be already embedded(and some get to view this from the lens of what is the big deal while others have to view this from the lens of why are you making my life hard. see the difference. fill the difference. gap it by being better. by caring. by not being the cause. by wanting the next person to feel seen feel heard feel loved feel connected and not disconnected. harmony would heal if the divide didn't exist. if we desired to peace together. to love one another. to brighten one another. to beautifully exist without hate.

four did you know's to wake up to.

did you know you are the sweetest melody.
did you know you are peace mixed with flowers.
did you know you are soul attractive.
did you know you make life much better.

the world waits impatiently for you to open your eyes and play. you are missed even if gone for two minutes. forget untrue stories told to you about you and breathe in all of you everyone wishes they could breathe in. you are fresh air.

***

you are air. fresh air. pure air. light air. deep air. intoxicating air. light. sweet. smokey. cool. and then there are elements of you that can't be identified that makes your air so alluring. so you. may the one who gets to breathe some of you deserve to taste test your magic energy.

you just need to know you are someone someone is thinking about right now right now. missing you right now. wanting you right now. and should they ever get to be anywhere near you may they never let you go and cherish you the way you deserve to be cherished. may they know they are lucky and do all that they can to never lose you.

may they do all they can to mirror you when you lose your way. when you even for a split second lose your knowing's to wake up to. they know this and you know this too. always fill in the gap of you if they don't bring the sun up with you.

six sometimes to examine deeply.

sometimes every part of you needs rest.
sometimes accepting yourself is uncomfortable.
sometimes you have to be your own sign.
sometimes they just can't see you for you.
sometimes going away means not coming back.
sometimes what you need isn't what you want.

the moment you let go of outside pressures and expectations of what others think and live for you and love for you then you fly. you really will fly.

***

i hope you know that even on days you don't feel your best or days that drag on or days you hear no validation or days you don't look forward to or days you feel small or days you are aimless or days that feel like years you will always always always make it where you need to be. just know it's more than okay to have daze in your days. life has those. but you have you. and that is beautiful. you are beautiful. you are enough of a beautiful soul to catch fire when cold. you are enough of a beautiful soul to be the light that needs to pierce through the cracks. you are enough of a beautiful soul to find what you need even if asking for it you avoid it because you want to be strong all by yourself)asking for help makes you stronger(. so begin. again. when you are ready to lift up and out. if right now you want to stay down stay down stay down stay down stay down and recoup. regroup. resoul. resoil. replant. recover. no use in pretending what your body is crying out for doesn't need to be tending to. attune to you. you'll be much clearer each time you do this. and repeat often.

33 lessons

accept. let go. forgive. reflect. unlearn. respond.
speak. listen. complete. intend. attend. notice.
practice. love. apologize. change. empathize.
lean in. prioritize. courage. accountability.
gratitude. joy. manifest. patience.
commitment. presence. grace.
understanding. consider.
believe. breathe.
give.

four irrefutable facts about you.

you are medicine.
you are godsend.
you are unforgettable.
you are lustrous.

and don't you forget it. many will vow to tear you down to avoid their own inner pain but you can't continue giving energy to those toxic people. herbs of you aren't for everybody. protect your medicine.

you are medicine. the sacred kind. not the over the counter in the front bay aisle or low enough to reach. no you are a best kept secret healers talk about in their books and potions. the kind that only comes around a few hundred years. you are a natural mystic. such a natural mystic. no one tells you this enough.

everyday is yours. to try. to try again. to do. to do over. to learn and unlearn. to apply and reapply and go in go in go in. but there is this hesitation. this delay. this wall to cause no friction or push back. you don't want to make waves. but oh the waves of you are what makes each day great. sometimes you are mighty and harsh and sharp and sometimes you're mellow and patient and rounded but you're always always always beautiful medicine. a dose of you takes the pain away. so dose to you and know that it's okay to crash into someone who needs a realty check or a racist check or a sexist check or a transphobic check or a xenophobic check or a anti-semitic check or any other kind of check that barriers people from being their full person. you are the check and the balance. use your power so everyone sees and feels and hears the hurricane of you. the healer of you. the harmony of you. the harvest of you. warrior stance and love on.

when you look in the mirror recite these words.

hello beautiful. i know i dodge you sometimes
)lots of times(but i'm working on that. i need you now
more than ever to hear that i am so proud of all
the things you do. the little things. the big
things. the heart in everything you do.
it feels like no one notices what
and who and why of you but i do. i do.
i see the magic of you. the wonder of you.
go after today and make sure each moment each
person senses the love in you. the pride in you. the
universe in you. you matter so deeply. i love you. xo.

***

you are the mirror. the dopest kind. imperfect kind with blemishes and cracks and dust particles that seem to never go away. and it's hard to see yourself because a mirror can't see itself. but there you are. i see you. i always have. what a sight you are. what a sight you are. and when you see you)you'll know when you see through(you'll see more endlessly more. untapped you. a reservoir spilling. and on the other side of what reflects back you'll ignite what needs igniting what needs warming what needs unearthing just by spending time with your ocean. don't neglect your ocean. don't fear your ocean. don't forget your ocean. don't forget you are ocean. vast. expansive. enriching. enriching. enriching. enriching not just others but you. so if you fall)you will(you catch yourself. breathe yourself and recite the words you need. recite the truths you need. recite your name to signature to mark to record your rain on water.

love language.

you shouldn't have to

teach someone how to love you.
teach someone how to treat you.
teach someone how to see you.
teach someone how to fill you.
teach someone how to hold you.

you should be with someone who wants to learn
all the ways about you. the wild about you. the
beauty of you. just by getting to know you. you
do not have to lecture but you are a seminar. the
syllabus of you is only intimidating to those with
lungs not ready for your depth and fine print.

you are a whole curriculum. a life-long syllabus. but the pages of you aren't lecture or dry or boring. you are an experience. engaging. life changing. your love language is the hardest to learn but the deepest worthiness. you shouldn't have to teach someone how to love you.

your heart and soul is doctorate level but your grace is on that spiritual level so down to earth. so humble. so open. but not just anyone can take your class. a class never before written as you update yourself daily. daily. what a daily prayer you are.

and if and when you enroll and take in and let in and open registration to your heart new stars emerge. new galaxies birth. new life finds ways to become when they couldn't find ways before. just the thought of being able to circuit your way is light enough to grow towards the sun. towards the love everyone yearns for.

what we all need.

someone to lean on.
someone to love us.
someone to hear us.
someone to trust us.
someone to open us.
someone to see us.
someone to balance us.
someone to relax us.
someone to rely on.
someone to witness us.
someone to celebrate us.
someone to affirm us.

love. let me tell you something. you are everything you need but you need someone. deserve someone. who knows you are everything. someone who won't take anything from you. someone who will receive all the giving you provide. all the soul you share. all the light you gift. love. you are everything everything. and an everything everything deserves everything everything not just anything anything. anyone will reach for you but not everyone can be for you what you already are for you. but that somebody is out there. that somebody is out there. speaking to your heart is the greatest experience. the greatest joy. seeing you light up and shimmer and glow and share what is happening in your world is a treat. such a treat. any failure any not-so-well any not-as-good-as-the-last is a set up to trick you to keep you from who you are meant to be. your voice is here. your voice is needed. the day is ready for you. the day has always been ready for you. this is your journey to become who you've been waiting for. come back to yourself. the world is just now catching up.

three types of safety you deserve.

emotional safety. all feelings are valid.
physical safety. body is respected.
psychological safety. full self is accepted.

a safe person. a safe place. a safe heart. a safe
love is essential for any relationship to thrive.
without it there is no vulnerability no intimacy
no trust no growth. you shouldn't have to be
on the defense as soon as you enter spaces
meant to hold you and water you and keep you
and deserve you.

***

take better care of yourself. don't let today be the day you are too harsh. love on yourself harder today.

and that can look how you need it to look like. how you need it to feel like. work backwards from what would balance you and decide how you need to feel there. and if you make it there great and if you don't make it there great. you ventured. you plotted. you breathed. you moved. there is no try without trying. so try. even if removing one piece of a piece of a piece gives a little peace that is victory. that is success. that is a start. being harsh just drives you further from the peace.

and in-between moments you will stumble into being critical. and when you do when you prick yourself with unkindess grace yourself. safe yourself. emotionally. physically. psychologically.

*the most beautiful goodbye
without saying goodbye.*

i don't want you to leave. stay with me until
the until never comes. five more minutes. let me
look at you a bit longer. so much wonder in the
details of you right before the before and after
the after. wherever you are going allow me to go
with you. to just sit in silence while you do whatever
it is you need to do. when you come back it will be
like you never left. my heart is beating crying out
for you to stay so stay. stay. your presence
always lifts me. is tomorrow here yet. when will
i see you again. you make me feel whole like
i'm home with you so home is wherever you are.
sleep here tonight. sleep. here. don't go. don't. go.
farewell is bittersweet. xo.

***

that heaviness. that tightness. that that. that whatever is taking root in your body is yearning for you to acknowledge it. yearning for you to tend to it even if tending means declaring something is there. what is that. where is that. that that. that lump in your throat or that ache in your back or that anxiety in your belly. that that. name that. address that. you'll feel better. body scan and be grateful for the temple you are in.

humans bloom because of you.

you bring goodness
to the lives of many.
you plant seeds in their soul.
humans bloom because of you.

the four best investments.

your heart. who you let in.
your health. what you let in.
your home. who you let stay.
your healing. what you let go.

and the moment you focus in on you and begin
to dig and pour and spill and give time back into
you you'll realize what is important. what isn't.
who you thought you wanted you won't want or
be held by the thought of them anymore and the
toxic it brought you. investing in you will be the
greatest thing you ever do for yourself.

you are then and now. calm and storm. the deep end the universe
warns people to beware of. hope you know this. hope you see this.
and never forget who you are among chaos.

***

you are your greatest investment. of course who you invest in get better. heal better. love better. take that same energy and invest it in you. don't always be last to get you some you. don't always be last to get you some you. place you in front on top in center first. and as you desire to put you back behind others to focus on others to deny your self priority remember you can't keep walking on fumes. you can't keep loving on drain. you can't give if empty. and if the world must wait the world will wait. the world will wait for you.

ten quiet whispers to always say out loud.

you will never be fully understood in the eyes
of people who can't look at the sun. lovers like you
leave love wherever you go. don't dim you down
because you think you deserve to shine less than
someone else. you're strong even if you think you're
being soft. being soft is the most beautiful touch anyone
touched by you will always remember. if anyone tells you
something that makes you feel insecure it isn't about you they
have a deep wound and project that insecurity on you. life is
colder when you don't bring your sun around. people will try so
hard to keep you from fulfilling what your heart needs so don't let
them stop you. right now right now someone is thinking of you.
thinking of just you.

***

being real is hard when being someone else or becoming what is trend is tempting. to go off path. to bask in the shadows of others. but stay. but stand. but ground. root in you. you know your truth. don't quiet your voice to tone it up to sound like what's hot right now. that fad will fall and you will be left standing. so stand. stand. stand. agree to yourself you will commit to you and be there for you when you just want to be someone else. how beautiful you are when no one can say you're like anyone else. for you. for you. for you are the mold. don't exchange your light for a faulty fuse. by standing strong you become the winds. you become the guide. you become who others look for on darkest nights.

the stars dance for you.

you are an honest love. a full love. a true love. a love love. a love love. a love so lovely the stars dance for you. just for you love. just for you love.

***what to do when stuff
doesn't go your way.***

look for the lesson.
don't force it to fit.
notice how you feel.
try another approach.
remove self doubt.
take deep breaths.
know it will be okay.
let go of control.
practice gratitude.

***

you are every wondrous word sense feeling experience energy all in one breath. all in one being. you are the impossible made possible. the just right. the just right. no need to convince anyone otherwise. you are all the planets stars galaxies universe blessing anyone and everyone who gets to feel any of your sunlight.

go tell someone you love them. not just in a passing by or quick text. but really really put some heart into your gratitude as to why you love them. send a voice memo. long text. get cut off on voicemail. draw it on their skin. whatever you can do. say it. share it. write a poem. write a book. paint or draw or sing. don't hold back. tomorrow ain't promised. get that love off your chest and spread it. you never know who needs a pick me up. we all need to get picked up even if we think we're alright.

sharing music is a love language.
it says:

listen to this. experience this. breathe this.
sense this. the vibration of this sound this
movement this wave reminds me deeply
of you. may it hit you how it hit me. may it
speak to your soul in ways my own words
are unable to unfold to you. that part
)that part(urged the very magic of you
into my being and lodged itself in my core.
the notes are dedicated to you. the rally cry
of the chorus to the bass to the beat to the
harmony wants to unite us. bind us. bring us
closer. did you listen. the rhythm of love
within each bar each break each lyric are
beautiful garden kisses on your neck.
kiss me back. kiss me back.

as soon as you get this.

choose yourself. not just the easy parts but the parts of you someone told you weren't lovable. parts of you someone nonchalantly threw your way and it became your worst nightmare. your worst flaw that was once your favorite sightsee. grab hold and reclaim and deny old messages entrance to your wonderland and guard your heart with beautiful word oil and deep clean massage and rub down rub down rub down all those tenses and stretches and tell you how much you love you. how much you are magic even if no one else sees. lift what may have been a curse and turn them into unopened gifts. the choice to love you is yours. so love you. give you the best homecoming lovecoming soulcoming that you've never had. lavender you. essential you. sage you. incense you. soak the flavors of you around you frequently. nowly. urgently. as soon as you get this. hold this to the light. your light. and depart from those people those places those panics that prevent you. that provoke you. that prove to you time and time and time and time and time and time again that they have overstayed their stay. that they get no more from your pour. they get no more from your stress. they get no more from your longing. now hold this to your heart and feel your own lown longing for you. your own beating for you. your own time asking for its time with you. reach back and re-dedicate what was dedicated for those that unearned you. reach back and re-dedicate what was dedicated for those that took from you. and remove that weight from your heart. let that pass. let that not be why you lose sleep. all that space you get back can be used for better use. all that space you get back can be used for choosing yourself. all that space you get back can be used for loving all and more all and more of you.

fifteen you don't have to's just for you.

you don't have to announce your healing.
you don't have to announce your resting.
you don't have to announce your loving.
you don't have to announce your crying.
you don't have to announce your hurting.
you don't have to announce your giving.
you don't have to announce your caring.
you don't have to announce your working.
you don't have to announce your scattering.
you don't have to announce your worrying.
you don't have to announce your anxieting.
you don't have to announce your craving.
you don't have to announce your wondering.
you don't have to announce your stopping.
you don't have to announce your anything.

you don't have to announce yourself. sometimes just being and living and breathing and wandering should be enough. to suffice. to provide you with grace and love you need. make sure you are taking good care of your needs. resting is an act of self love and an act of self treason if you don't prioritize it. so take a break. gather yourself. and don't give another second to stuff that has been keeping you away from yourself. because some of us have no choice but to have to always announce. and prep. and shout. and maintain. and tiptoe. and caution. and diminish. and benefit the doubt to. in order to come home safe. to not get shot. to not get shot. to not get shot. to not get hashtagged. this isn't back to normal by any means. justice has sadly been a life-long battle for some of us while others get to focus on wondering what all the justice fighting is all about.

be prepared

to advocate for yourself.
to sometimes stand alone.
to accept rejection.
to lose close relationships.
to be misunderstood.

wherever you are in your life you will face
)and continue to face(obstacles. you can
run away or run towards. lessons reside in
both. up to you which will make you better
and which won't help you grow. don't get
in the way of yourself. don't block your love.

***

you are the stand and the standing. the rain and the reign. the speech and the speechless. you'll never be as good for someone as you already are. you'll only and always be greater and someone's best someone. someone's best someone.

accept yourself as is. love yourself as is. strive only to be you and not the you someone else has drawn up in their minds for you to live up to. there is always room to grow and learn and unlearn and be a better person but not at the expense of being a character in the life of someone else. it is up to you to decide and grow from there.

twelve signs you're in a toxic relationship.

narcissistic. all about them. never about you.
always challenging. uphill battles. rarely easy.
feeling unworthy. diminished sense of value.
standards drop. have to lower expectations.
lack of communication. constant avoidance.
trust isn't there. no reliability or confidence.
hostile environment. endlessly tense. aggressive.
draining. energy is heavily negative and tiring.
all they do is take. there is no give. control issues.
growth is stunted. stuck and going nowhere.
left picking up the pieces. the only one trying.
blame. made to feel everything is your fault.

in your heart. in your aura. in your everything.
you know you deserve better. go where better is.

you make people want to leave their old life and grow with you in yours. because you are rich in life and love and anyone lucky enough to get your love would drop all the bad all the toxic and strive to earn your good natured soul.

whatever relationship you are in. professional. personal. platonic. romantic. no one should constantly treat you like you are dispensable. because without you they would be soul-less. heart-less. love-less. you could be anywhere and with anyone working for any organization at any school or program. you are a beautiful powerhouse. just be cautious no one takes advantage of you and your hues and your beliefs and your ideas. they better pay close attention before you're gone and move on to somewhere someplace someone who would do anything to keep you safe.

three reasons you are really angry.

you are sad.
you are scared.
you are hurt.

you have every right to be angry. enraged.
tension and heat and red and tightness grip
you and you could cry you're so mad. so
frustrated. but under that. under the current
of it are truer emotions. deeper flooding.
don't deny yourself the ability to check-in
what's at the heart of your anger. go there.
heal there. get better there. resolve there.

***

you are a loving warrior. down to fight for those you care for. down to love how people deserve to be loved. you are the perfect combination of water and fire. no one can extinguish or drown you love.

when you find yourself angry check in with yourself. what is under it. how are you really feeling and why. why. why. ask yourself why. your behavior shows anger but your body may tell you something else as well. the quicker you determine the root the quicker you can speak to what you need and how you can be supported or received. either way it's okay to be angry. wonder if there is something else going on. but do not be so quick to fix. this isn't the task. the task is to be quick to probe not be quick to get out of. there is a difference. understanding your roots is a process.

effort is a love language.
it says:

i'm trying. i'm giving. i'm besting. putting
my all my everything my energy into this.
this is hard but staying and pushing through
will be worth it. because you are worth it.
you are worthy. before i was kind of in.
kind of not prepared. kind of avoiding.
that wasn't effort. that was immaturity.
i'm learning. and you don't deserve
anything less than full. determined to
show up and exert and do and grit and
unfold and best person. your person.
not performance. not facade. opening
myself for whatever may come so at least
i can say i did what was in my control.
what is meant won't miss.
giving until i have no give left.

***

if you aren't going to even go all in there is no reason to step in in the first place. it is one thing to be cautious it is another to have motive knowing it will only be one-sided. some people are like that. don't be like that. don't be the one who says the right things just to say them. feel what is feeling and convey that. express what has to be said instead of what you think would be good to be expressed. the honest person acknowledges the rise as rise and the fall as fall not to trick but to true. and truth is worth every ounce of effort.

goodness grows towards you.

you are the sign you've been looking for. the heart you've been praying for. the love you've been seeking for. the beautiful soul someone is yearning for. by focusing on yourself you become a magnet and goodness grows towards you.

the world feels you no matter what you do.

don't fixate on changing yourself in hopes that someone you think you want will notice. work on yourself for yourself and the right one will sense the beauty you already have and need. if you change for someone else it won't last. you won't last. decide what you need to be better and feel yourself shift without worrying if the world notices. it does. the world feels you no matter what you do.

so you take notice. on how every little thing you do ripples. how every slight tilt causes a reaction. notice when you withdraw who comes back. notice when you water who brings their own bucket.

so you take you. wherever you need to go. to be. to see. to breathe. to think. to patient. to consider all that needs your consideration. maybe what you think you wanted will remain. maybe what you think you wanted will distant memory. allow. and by allowing you accept and detach from what won't be and appreciate what is supposed to be. but if you think you changing will bring a certain person a certain event a certain opportunity it will. but not the exact person or the exact event or the exact opportunity you have in mind. what's in heart for you will come to you)already has come to you(when you are ready to grasp it. when you are ready to have it. when you are ready to acknowledge it. you just can't shape it how you need it to be shaped. it won't fit. you just can't shape them how you need them to be shaped. they won't fit. your change has to be free from force. free from maybe. free from their waiting. when you change for you)your authentic you(what comes will come and be better for you because you are better for you.

routine.

don't forget to applaud yourself.
transitions. events. moments.
big or small. it doesn't matter.
celebrate you. be proud of you.
water you. enjoy you.

***

you deserve to be celebrated for all the little all the big all the in-between. keep doing the dang thing. someone is watching. you are watching. in the front row of your own life be the first to toot your own horn from time to time. enjoy yourself.

long week but you did it. you fucking did it. you at first were hesitant and didn't think you would make it but you did. no one around sometimes to applaud you but damnit applaud you. reward you. celebrate you. doesn't matter if they don't see what you did. you did what you did and are better for it. be proud of you.
i am proud of you. i love you. thank you.

truly. i mean that. i know what it is like to do and not be done for. to best and be averaged for. i wish more humans knew how to treat humans less transactional. more emotional. more thoughtful. more like sacred gifts. highly honored because their attention could be anywhere else. your attention could be anywhere else. and what you sacrifice what you lend yourself to what you hour upon hour upon hour should bow to you. should smile to you. should recognize they wouldn't be as bold or as coveted or as successful without you. so thank you. the deepest thank you.

emotional labor is cancelled.
here is why.

emotional labor is unpaid.
emotional labor is invisible.
emotional labor is unappreciated.
emotional labor is disproportionate.

you do this to help keep others in their comfort. in their happy. in their content. while keeping you uncomfortable. unhappy. stressed. tired. drained. out of balance. keeping you emotionally depleted and emotionally invisible. doing the work of many when it shouldn't be your burden at all to carry. you have done enough. so rest. let them figure it out. or pay you hella extra.

don't post on your website that you believe in equity and treat people inequitable. don't post your mission statement with the word inclusivity and you say there aren't any qualified BIPOC to hire. don't create content with folks of color on it to prove you have students of color on your campus but have no targeted intention to retain support and nurture families of color. stop relying on BIPOC to vision strategize deliver work or add diversity responsibilities to their plate without a huge bump in their salary when their primary responsibility is to already emotionally labor being one of few to absorb countless microaggressions. put money where your mouth is and invest and budget and prioritize diversity equity and inclusion policies practices and procedures into every aspect of your organization. this applies to relationships, too. imagine having to speak on behalf of your lived experience your traumas your identities over and over and over like you are always the case study. imagine. imagine. imagine.

ten all right's that make you human.

it's all right to hold onto somebody.
it's all right to let somebody in.
it's all right to take time to grieve loss.
it's all right to struggle to get out of bed.
it's all right to miss someone deeply.
it's all right to be sad and not know why.
it's all right to talk through your feelings.
it's all right to wish for what you don't have.
it's all right to sometimes care less.
it's all right to love to love to love.

***

it's all right to experience whatever it is you are experiencing. don't think you are alone. you are never alone. don't expect yourself to always be 100 percent when it's too difficult to get cents at times and you just need time to catch your breath and refuel and refill. take whatever time you need do not succumb to thinking you have to show up with a smile if all you want to do is frown and sad and break and be alone. just don't stay there. come up and remember it takes a village. and the village is not the same without a soul like you.

take this with you.

you are everything someone forgot to say.
be proud of everything you've become.

***

you are all the right words and all the right feelings.
what doesn't come from others give yourself.

i know you want to hear that you're doing a great job and that you are amazing at all that you do and that you are loved beyond measure and that you are so beautiful so beautiful. and when those words don't come or actions don't follow you question your security your heart your presence. but today don't do that. know for a fact you are everything someone forgot to say. be proud of everything you've become in spite of the language people have failed to speak your way.

the sky is whatever color you want it to be.

you are the constant when there is unpredictability.
a force that pulls that pulls that pulls in a world that is
addicted to pushing. clouds clear because of you. the sky
is whatever color you want it to be.

two reminders.

let you in.
protect your heart.

***

don't wall yourself in while needing to keep others out.
don't wall yourself in while needing to keep others out.
don't wall yourself in while needing to keep others out.
don't wall yourself in while needing to keep others out.
don't wall yourself in while needing to keep others out.
don't wall yourself in while needing to keep others out.
don't wall yourself in while needing to keep others out.
don't wall yourself in while needing to keep others out.
don't wall yourself in while needing to keep others out.
don't wall yourself in while needing to keep others out.
don't wall yourself in while needing to keep others out.
don't wall yourself in while needing to keep others out.
don't wall yourself in while needing to keep others out.
don't wall yourself in while needing to keep others out.
don't wall yourself in while needing to keep others out.
don't wall yourself in while needing to keep others out.
don't wall yourself in while needing to keep others out.
don't wall yourself in while needing to keep others out.
don't wall yourself in while needing to keep others out.
don't wall yourself in while needing to keep others out.
don't wall yourself in while needing to keep others out.
don't wall yourself in while needing to keep others out.
don't wall yourself in while needing to keep others out.
don't wall yourself in while needing to keep others out.
don't wall yourself in while needing to keep others out.
don't wall yourself in while needing to keep others out.
don't wall yourself in while needing to keep others out.

full stop.

if you can't be you
)all of your magic self(
don't be with them.
period.

you are an old soul.

you are an old soul
that believes in
chivalry. romance.
and love.

***

that is the richness of you. the riches of you. the wealth of you.
that classic. that vintage. that style. that trademark. that
uncomparable. that uncompromising. you. that soul. you. cannot
be mistaken but you have been misloved. one too many times.
once is too much. more than once they must not know who
you are. the ore in you the world in you the glow in you. if they
overlook you they miss out on everything. as you are everything.
the good times that they could have had. they come to their senses
when their moment has dissolved once they have chosen another.
and that is okay. you move on. you care on. you heart on. you
have always been destined for the stars beyond the stars.

souls like you love the sweetest as you need nothing added.
you are the perfect amount of honey and water. sometimes
you are more water. sometimes you are more honey.

love to you isn't a game. isn't to mess around. love to you
is sacred. a most sacred gift. to open. to hold. to give.
to romance. to forever. to anything for. and that
)old soul(is how you were named. a heart
like yours. after those deep like you.
after those who shine like you.
after those who love like you.

ten keys to a meaningful life.

find your why.
re-define success.
practice gratitude.
give back.
laugh more.
love deep.
water relationships.
accept yourself.
value others.
know your worth.

***

anyone who knows you)the real you(is beyond lucky. they get to experience wonder in real life in the shape of you. that is true love. the kind that starts and stops your heart all at once. what a wonder you are.

never make yourself small. never again. that was practice enough. now lean in. lean in. lean in. into all that power you have been marinating. all that voice you've been quieting. all that leadership you've been hiding. no time to let others take a mantle that never was theirs in the first place. now. now. now more than ever. manifest and rise and speak into what was a mirage of terror and fear. you are ready. they ain't ready. seize the rest of your days and watch the world change because of your light.

one part of your story.

experience taught you.
hurt raised you.
neither defined you.

***

the story of you is powerful. and being who you are you don't think it is. you don't see the profound. you don't see the special. you don't see any reason to think it worth sharing compared to others. but their story is theirs. and your story is yours. don't discount who you are and what you have been through and what you have grown through and what you yet to bloom through. the story of you is powerful. it has all the fixings for wanting to know what comes next. you are the hero on a journey. the regular with incredible untapped powers. the magic one who touches souls without trying without knowing without understanding that you water seeds that sit dormant in others. but they don't grow without you. without you they go along as they go along. aimlessly. but you ignite but you spark but you set fires in humans to want more. to strive more. to keep going. you have gone through some things. some tough obstacles. easy for some. tougher for others. everyone has their own path. and through your hurt through your pain through your experience you unveil an essence. a been there before even if you haven't been exactly there you remember the feeling. and you didn't let that part of your story stop you. you didn't let it define you as all of you. the story of you is so damn powerful. this time when you tell it this time when you share it this time when you unpack it know that. know that. know that. the story of you is powerful. the story of you is powerful. the story of you is powerful. the story of you is powerful. the story of you is powerful. the story of you is powerful.

keep their name on your lips.

loss is a part of life.
and losing a loved one
hurts bone deep.
grieve slowly.
hate the world if you must.
you will deny and repress.
feel angry and depressed.
grow through it. then accept.
they may be gone but remember:
they are always with you as long
as you keep their name on your lips.

your greatest affirmation.

you are your greatest affirmation.

let them.

they will critique you. let them.
they will gossip. let them.

you know who you are.
bright lights allow negativity
and never become it.

two secrets from the universe to practice.

love you more.
don't sweat small stuff.

***

practice these vital secrets.
become these vital secrets.

it may seem trivial and it might sound too simple. but trivial simple things can sometimes be the details needed to fill us in. to whole us in. so try it. why not. remix them as you see fit. what does loving you more look like. what does loving you more feel like. what does loving you more sound like. how can you keep the small stuff from seeping in. how can you keep the small stuff from determining your reactive response. how can you keep the small stuff from causing more harm if it is indeed harmful. do you know. how would you know. the best way to determine all of this really takes time. really takes you. really shouldn't be so hard. but it is. and you know why. because all of us aren't perfect. all of us have things that prick us that we've told ourselves we wouldn't let prick us again. so do what you need to figure you out. how to turn less red the next time someone says something or something doesn't go your way that interrupts your peace. perhaps you strive for a gradient. perhaps you flow into orangeish hues but revert back to a kind of red and notice that and take a breath and dim down into a somewhat yellow. perhaps that is a way of loving you more. perhaps that is not letting the small stuff grip. perhaps. on you to determine. on you to suffice. on you to wrestle with secrets that shouldn't be secret. on you to find how to better. and help others better. not always directly. but always by acting. by showing that if you can de-escalate and vibrate higher. anyone can. anyone can.

considerate.

heal your wounds
before you jump
into the wounds
of others.

***

to know what triggers you is a love language.
it says:

i've been here before. i've felt here before. i thought it was gone
but it's still there. still festering when i believed it unlatched from me.
i acknowledge its presence and do not want it to do what it used to
do to me what it used to do to others i love dearly what it used to
make me think about myself. i recognize you now in advance. and
take back the energy the power the conditioning
to continue to heal myself. to care myself. to aware that i do
not cause the harm that was done to me onto anyone else
so not to wound them so not to pass burden from me
onto them without knowing it. i won't always catch
myself. i won't always see my actions until after
the action but if i can catch myself in the act
more than i catch myself after the act then
that is beautiful. that is progress. that is
what i am working on.

love on some you.

if you rely on the love of someone else to lead a meaningful life then you will forever be at their mercy. so love on some you.

everevolving love.

love is vibration.
a connection of the highest
frequency. we can try to wrap
our minds to define it. but love
is everevolving. constantly
transforming.

move with love.
feel with love.
grow with love.
dive into its rhythm.
breathe in love.
become the vibration.
become full.
become love.
let it cover all of you.

can't be loved separately.

all parts of us want to be seen. no desire no ambition no ask to be made a big deal. all parts of us simply want to be noticed. to be acknowledged. that is it. that is all that matters. to ignore even one ounce of who we are or what we reveal is to weaken our humanity. no part of us is accessory. we can't be loved separately.

***

you can't be loved separately. you can't be compartmentalized. you can't be halved. you can't be less thanned. you can't be spliced. those that would want to do that to you are just trying to do to you what was done to them or)always or(they want to barricade you from all your mightiness. all your nature that at its max is impenetrable. so go on. disappear them from your gaze. disappear them from your what's ahead. disappear them and take all of you with you in determination. in light. in bold. in humility. because when you do that more and more and more and more and more courage no longer is a word. courage becomes synonymous with you.

stay close to hearts that care like yours.

i. the beauty in me honors the beauty in you.
that gets communicated that gets delivered
that gets sent without words. your energy
speaks and that is divine communication.

ii. no one is as thoughtful as the one who thinks two needs ahead.
the one who considers moods that will arise that haven't been
moods yet. the way you cater to the soul is like walking
to water already full. getting more to prepare to give more
to love more to be what you know you would want when thirsty.

iii. when they come to you you sometimes big sigh because you
yourself haven't had time to unwind. to rest. to exhale. to unravel.
to play back what happened in your day. but you make space. you
make room. you open your soul and let them in to breathe. they
breathe better because of you. they feel better because of you. they
love better because of you. just by simply opening up. by making
time)no one makes time like you(the air you provide is always
crisp.

iv. to know there is a you is to know pure wonder.
no explanation needed. just seeing you be is
beautiful grounding. beautiful breathing.
beautiful praising. gratitude for you.
always always gratitude for you.
to stay close to hearts that care like yours is all
the inspiration all the muse all the love desired to be.

for things to grow water must fall.

weep often.
not in sadness.
but in celebration.

for things to grow
water must fall.

***

it's okay to boundary.
it's okay to reinforce.
it's okay to say no.
it's okay to push pause.
it's okay to be alone.
it's okay to want more.
it's okay to keep to yourself.
it's okay to slow.
it's okay to uncertain.
it's okay to wait until until.
it's okay to change your mind.
it's okay to protect your heart.

the world around you can be a reflection of the world inside you. whether you feel connected or detached, how you treat someone is a choice. and whatever rattles within we all have our own internal battles. don't wage a war on someone else because you feel like you are losing yours.

cry into the wind.

cry into the wind
and taste river tears
for the salt
in your eyes
are magic pearls.

let the air
return
your natural
gemstones
back
to your ocean skin.

***

wherever you are. stop where you are.
check in. check in. check in. check in.
how is your heart. honestly.
what do you need. are you getting what you need.
are you. are you. what is in your control.
right now. breathe. again. and again.
do you feel lighter. breathe. again.
do you feel your light. breathe.
again what needs to again.
visit what needs a visit.
establish a time a window a always
and do that. daily. daily. daily.
without delay. without telling yourself
you're too busy for yourself.
wherever you are. stop where you are.
check in. check in. check in. check in.

four parts of you to always protect.

protect your heart.
protect your energy.
protect your love.
protect your space.
protect your magic.

there is nothing selfish)ever selfish(about needing to keep yourself safe. to protect yourself from harm. too often people think this is self-serving and self-centered. it is. the most beautiful and positive thing you could ever do is to treat yourself gently and kind. don't apologize for protecting your soul.

***

when you protect your heart you're protecting all parts of you others tried to shatter and take. you aren't obligated to forfeit your self love. you are obligated to reinforce it.

it's okay to feel joy when all around you is chaotic. it's okay to turn on your light even if you just want to sit in the dark. even if for a few breaths. come up and relish and smile and celebrate and then armour and defend and put in work. you're entitled to some feel good. it is necessary to sustain yourself.

purpose.

we must burn to ignite our aptitude to love fully
to live passionately. to understand who we are at core.
be curious enough to care about our impact on others
and take action to leave this place better than we found it.

five post-it notes to place on your wall of healing.

i know you are hurting.
stay in there. grow there.
become stronger there.
heal there.

four gems to remember
when feeling unsteady.

remember your roots. you are deep.
remember your power. you are strong.
remember your voice. you are unique.
remember your sacred. you are valued.

you can do all things. be all things. it is only
a matter of how far you want to travel. how
much gold you want to create. always know
you are everything you need and more.

***

whether you are down or up or having difficulty naming how you're feeling or if on autopilot. you are everything. incredible. amazing. essential. important. needed. necessary. noticed. noble. kind. you are a shining star. shine on. shine on.

a letter to you.

dear you. come. please sit awhile. will you. let us talk about your pain. but today. just today. let me go first. then i will be happy to listen to yours. i don't like to take up space but i'm learning to reclaim my space. to process my process. and not apologize all the time for my need to do some digging. for my need to center me sometimes. for my need to show up for me more. this can no longer be a one-sided dynamic. i can no longer just be a sounding board and get nothing in return. laying that foundation laying those norms laying those agreements)for me(is essential instead of having to deal with not having any time for me. this is not for you to feel blame or shame or guilt)tho you have every right to feel how you feel(but that can't stop you from holding space for me. allowing me equal time. i've given you so much. let me get some too. healing outloud isn't the same as healing inloud. i am master of inner. my inner. getting better at inner. but for too long when i have tried to verbalize i get shut down shut out scrutinized. this isn't about you. not now. don't turn this around. i haven't even gotten to what needs to be gotten to. please stay seated. please stay open. please do not respond. i need to get this all out. forgive me if my words speak quicker than my thoughts and i ramble. let me meander. and if i don't make sense. if you are confused. if you don't understand. that's okay. this is my cleansing. my process. my time.

what i need to say is...

)say what you need to say(.

five seconds of advice.

breathe deeper.
you will get the
clarity you have
been looking for.

sometimes flowers don't want you to be gentle.

sometimes
flowers
don't
want you
to be
gentle.

>

cutting parts of what doesn't serve you is what will actually make you grow faster because you were keeping yourself and stunting yourself from all the good ends by holding onto all those dead ends.

five when's to remember.

when the world turns its back on you and you feel all alone.
when no one will listen and you're on your own.
when the cold pavement is your only pillow.
when your heart is crushed and you fall numb to your knees.
when you are at your lowest.

even lovers must rise from the ashes.

***

you should have the audacity to fearlessly be you. to know as much about your shadows as you do of your light. you should tall if they try to make you feel small. you should find solace on your search for silent retreat. you should know deep down your feelings matter and your feelings are real and your feelings are welcome. you should prepare for your upward healing. because what comes down must go up to deep with air. to refresh. to sun. to warm. to mix and nutrient. what feels like brutal challenge and never ending sorrow will turn as the tides pull with the moon. back to shore. then back to water. back to shore. then back to water. in and out is a natural rotation. a normal cycle. a necessary function. both parts teach you a lot about yourself. both parts rise you. both parts are you.

***the most beautiful good morning
without saying good morning.***

there you are. there you are. you crossed my mind throughout the night and i have been waiting to tell you. waiting to get the chance to see your smile. feel that smile. finally. seeing you is sun rising. grand rising. my goodness the honey on your bones blushes through your skin. may whatever is meant for you come to you today. hope your heart is balanced and rested. you are my happy thought. stay awhile. let's connect.

***

you are someone's happy thought.
someone's hope. someone's prayer.
someone's dream. someone's everything.
and you don't even know it. don't even believe it.
don't even think it. take that away from your mind
and leave it as far away as possible. never for one second
think otherwise. by just showing up
you are someone's love language.
someone's affirmation. someone's gift.
someone's touch. someone's water.
someone's lifeline.

center you more.

quiet the noise of others.
learn to listen to yourself.

***

you were always meant to live like flowers exist.
wild. untamed. drenched in sun. growing. growing.
growing towards the sky. always in a constant bloom.
not for the entertainment or amusement or enjoyment
or will of others. but for yourself. how you please.
where you please. why you please. with the ability
to uproot and deep wherever you choose.

people have opinions and words that will take you in a direction away from where you should go. out of the goodness of their heart or the badness of their blindspots take what they say with a grain of salt and decide what is best for you. feel what is best for you. don't ever feel like you have to take what anyone says as the only way or the way without measuring it against your own checks and balances. if you always go by what others think then every step of the way you will need verification and validation and will begin to lose confidence in your own decision making. this doesn't mean shut people out. this means don't shut yourself out. this means learn to work backwards and start by asking yourself what do you think. what do you want. trust trust trust what follows will come with a lesson that proves you are able. proves you don't have to be perfect. proves that your voice should always cut through rather than be background. center you more. center you more.

double double standard.

judging others for something you do.
judging others for something you do.
judging others for something you do.
judging others for something you do.
judging others for something you do.
judging others for something you do.
judging others for something you do.
judging others for something you do.
judging others for something you do.
judging others for something you do.
judging others for something you do.
judging others for something you do.
judging others for something you do.
judging others for something you do.
judging others for something you do.
judging others for something you do.
judging others for something you do.
judging others for something you do.
judging others for something you do.
judging others for something you do.
judging others for something you do.
judging others for something you do.
judging others for something you do.
judging others for something you do.
judging others for something you do.
judging others for something you do.
judging others for something you do.

***

notice when you do this.

five answers to questions you never ask // keep asking.

follow your heart.
listen to your intuition.
the risk will be the reward.
if it doesn't work you tried.
you should trust yourself.

***

is it the answer you fear or the question you fear. is it what others may think or is it what you may think. is it too far away or is it too close up. is it never going to happen or is it on its way towards you. if you had three minutes and thirty seconds)the average length of a song(and that is all you had left before your opportunity closed for good. what would you do. what was your answer just now. did you change it. what was your gut reaction. what words did your heart speak. did your mind take over. ask yourself again. ask yourself again. ask yourself again.

self-awareness is a love language.
it says:

this is your home. this is your haven. i know when you are off. i know when you are misaligned. i know what keeps you up. i know what brings you joy. listen to the energy the vibration the echo within. worry less about everyone else. everyone else matters but you matter too. you outsourced your love and relied on others. resource your love and fill your inner being. come back to you. come back to you. converge where you feel spacious and settle in settle in. occupy that heart and demand your own attention. this is your home. this is your haven. you impact the best in those around you when you best in your own you. when you inventory and internal and mindfully heartfully soulfully wonder what you do that ripples out to others. what you do reaches out to others. what you do adds to or diminishes others. you don't intend to injure others but if you do you take accountability and apologize authentically and change your behavior willfully as your intention is to do good. to make good. to love good. be more gentle. be more soft. be more forgiving of you. so much growth in you no one else can deeply see. the patience to be where you are now how you feel now how you heal now are the beautiful waves of you crashing.

you deserve this kind of love. II

whatever it is you close your eyes and hope for. a serenity prayer remixed from your lips direct into your version of god's ear and without you having to say anything your being will appear with more than your wildest dream gave you vision for. a kind love. an understanding love. a faith worth believing in love. the kind that when it happens you already said your i-love-you's in a past lifetime. because this love coming)this love you may already have(crawls just at the surface and sits in sight playing music only lovers know. may it hit and crash beautifully over and over and over again.

***

you are not an almost you are an everything. and any person that makes you feel like an option has no business entering your heart and mind.

trust is a love language.
it says:

*i just don't let anyone in. not because i am
picky or unavailable or closed off. because
i can. this means you have one chance which
will tell me if you are like the others. my heart
has been through a lot)too many a lot's(that
makes earning my love more challenging.
if i open up even a little bit i am giving part
of a window into me not everyone can peer
into. i am counting on you to hold this bond.
hold this connection. hold this chemistry.
relying on someone is hard. my walls
are down for you.*

.

four things you are entitled to do. II

start over.
take time to process.
reject advice.
change your love language.

twelve roses to give yourself more often.

give more grace.
give more time.
give more love.
give more passion.
give more space.
give more patience.
give more compassion.
give more energy.
give more dedication.
give more you.
give more.
give.

you're only misunderstood if you attach your worth onto what others think about you. let others flounder to box you in. let you float and flourish outside in the wild where you belong.

***

let what's on your mind go and give it some time off. be present with yourself and focus on filling you with harmony. if that is a joy ride then ride. if it is a song then sing. if it is writing then write. if it is a sit just sit. don't lose sleep over small stuff that won't matter in a few days. all that stress isn't yours. let it go.

and when you give yourself what you need in that moment it is as if you have given yourself a lifetime of permission slips to deploy the universe to help you let go and make room for what better serves you.

ten small and big things you should be hella proud of.

facing your fears.
moving to another place.
saying no when you felt pressured to say yes.
promoting yourself.
asking for support.
listening to your intuition.
stepping out of your comfort zone.
addressing a not-a-big-deal that was actually a deep trauma.
speaking against hate speech.
learning how to be anti-racist.

***

there is always time to celebrate and appreciate and acknowledge the work that you are doing. the work that you are. being you isn't always easy)most people think you have no problems under the sun(but they don't know)no one ever really knows(so triumph and cheer and honor all that you are. but do not pat yourself on the back if what you do is on the backs and advantages of others. there is no pride or boast about the oppression of another being. so if part of your work isn't focusing on and considering and wondering what liberation for all folks looks like then delay applause and consider what work you have left to do. what voice isn't being heard. what story is being omitted. you cannot check a box when people are being boxed in intentionally. this doesn't mean you cannot rejoice or be proud. this is a reminder that no being should ever be made to feel less than because someone else is intimidated by their light. incremental change is still change but it speeds up with soul work.

five things you can't mess up.

your commitment to growing.
your commitment to those you bring into and up in this world.
your commitment to responding to unfairness.
your commitment to leaning into discomfort.
your commitment to leaving this place better than you found it.

***

maybe you haven't committed to this yet. maybe you have other commitments. maybe just one. maybe you are still trodding on whatever it is you are trodding on that needs all the attention you have right now. but when you have a moment to set aside write something down. write all the things down. put in writing what you hold in your mind. and timeline it. forever what needs to be forevered and deadline whatever needs to be deadlined and future whatever needs to be futured and present whatever needs to be presented. and return to your list. as much or as little as you need. pin it somewhere in sight or out of sight. these can be anchors for when you feel you are being blown around and have nothing to ground you. nothing to lighthouse you. nothing to breathe with you. what are the non-negotiables. the most important important that must get done get practiced get watered for you to feel fulfilled. for you to commit to you. perhaps they become mantra perhaps they become tatted perhaps they become inspiration to fill your heart in. the sixth thing you can't mess up is messing up. it's okay to be messy.

remember.

life is not a race.
life is not a race.
life is not a race.
go at your pace.
go at your pace.
go at your pace.

***

you will feel pulled to pull into something that isn't ready. pulled into someone who isn't yours. pulled into somewhere you think you belong. pulled into pulling when you should just be noticing. observing. wondering. archiving. unlearning. in this moment you don't even have to push. you don't have to push. you don't have to push. pushing is too closely linked with too much energy you may not have or want to give. that is okay. you will know when you need to push because you know you. but when it comes to pulling for the sake of pulling without a purpose keep a recording of when that occurs. bring it to your awareness. question it. sink your wiseness into the bed of it. resist the urge or else you fall into patterns you are needing to let go of. producing doesn't always grant good fruits. perhaps the fruit you currently now have hasn't been eaten or the juices are still freshly on your palate. life is not a race. you do not need to compete. you do not need to rush.

don't overthink. overfeel.

don't overthink. overfeel.
and let go let go so your emotions
say what your jealous mind conceals.

***

overthinking is okay. you are human. but if you do too much of it. if you rely too heavily on it. all you will be able to do is think. all you will be able to do is further delay. all you will be able to do is think yourself out of acting. think yourself out of feeling. think yourself out of being. but if you can sometimes overfeel and let there be an adjustment let there be a changing of the guard let there be feeling instead of just thinking then you will come back to you. you will return to the heartquarters that have been evacuated. you will allow much needed emotional reign emotional rain emotional insight that drops you into where you've needed to be. where you've avoided. where you can go now. go there now. breathe there now. this may sound repetitive but that is the importance of reminders. they have to come back again and again so they aren't forgotten. so you don't forget you. all the parts of you must be considered. and re-considered. give your mind a break. give your heart its turn. your thoughts have been on overdrive allow your emotions the road. roll your anxiety and your tension and your desire to brain this down and feel and feel and feel and feel and feel and feel and feel and feel.

i hope today deserves you.

i hope today deserves you.
i hope today earns you.
i hope today is worthy of your presence.
i hope today appreciates you.
i hope today heals you.
i hope today is gentle with your heart.
i hope today nourishes you.
i hope today inspires you.
i hope today is respectful of your pace.
i hope today builds you.
i hope today affirms you.
i hope today is thankful for your light.
i hope today softens you.
i hope today empowers you.
i hope today is better to your soul.
i hope today blankets you.
i hope today admires you.
i hope today is gracious of your desires.
i hope today follows you.
i hope today hears you.
i hope today is amenable to your cries.
i hope today acknowledges you.
i hope today honors you.
i hope today is cherishing all of you.
i hope today heartens you.
i hope today loves you.
i hope you find these words and breathe them in
)you will when you need them most(so save this.
save you. i hope today is good to you.

don't lose yourself chasing after others.

don't lose yourself chasing after others.
don't lose yourself chasing after others.
don't lose yourself chasing after others.
don't lose yourself chasing after others.
don't lose yourself chasing after others.
don't lose yourself chasing after others.
don't lose yourself chasing after others.
don't lose yourself chasing after others.
don't lose yourself chasing after others.
don't lose yourself chasing after others.
don't lose yourself chasing after others.
don't lose yourself chasing after others.
don't lose yourself chasing after others.
don't lose yourself chasing after others.
don't lose yourself chasing after others.
don't lose yourself chasing after others.
don't lose yourself chasing after others.
don't lose yourself chasing after others.
don't lose yourself chasing after others.
don't lose yourself chasing after others.
don't lose yourself chasing after others.
don't lose yourself chasing after others.
don't lose yourself chasing after others.
don't lose yourself chasing after others.
don't lose yourself chasing after others.
don't lose yourself chasing after others.
don't lose yourself chasing after others.
don't lose yourself chasing after others.
don't lose yourself chasing after others.
don't lose yourself chasing after others.
don't lose yourself chasing after others.
don't lose yourself chasing after others.

no longer accepting. III

the same mistakes.
the same patterns.
the same apologies.
the same answers.
the same games.

you are a new new. in your next chapter. but you're not one to close and never look back you keep open and return to learn from and honor where you have been even if where you've been makes you take a hard look at yourself so much so you)in the past(have turned away. even in those old pages you have gems and embers of what makes you you that can't be forgotten. and in your learnings and your tales and adventures there is a hard stop. a road that no longer accepts passage. no longer has vacancy. no longer holds an audience for. or tolerates that doesn't serve you. it may have taken volumes of heartache to get here but here you are. standing firm. standing ground. standing. standing. standing.

***

the human in you is still wired to go back and allow old behaviors old comforts old resources old desires and benefit of the doubts in. the task now is to notice when you revert. before you revert. notice when you think before you do. so that you catch yourself because you are the only one with you twenty four seven. you take you with you even when you forget about you. but this time and the next time and the time after that make it about sticking to what you want versus crumbling for someone else when you do not want to crumble)there is a difference(.

fourteen carries to wear in sun ight.

carry love.
carry kindness.
carry confidence.
carry dignity.
carry hope.
carry gratitude.
carry respect.
carry ancestors.
carry values.
carry humility.
carry patience.
carry beauty.
carry passion.
carry whatever will remind you of what
magic is made of. and that's always you.

no quote will ever capture the pure of you. because you are a poem. and poems are never meant to be captured. they are meant to be experienced. and you. you are the most beautiful experience. the most beautiful experience.

***

home is what you carry with you. in you. around you. it is a fragrance you spray on the small of your neck or the pocket of your shirt. the locket on your bracelet or the memory in your mind. home is you. always you. wherever you are everyone wants to be. home. what magic you are. what magic you are.

when you know you have learned and grown.

energy moves on. that person that job that trip
that feeling that gripped you for so so so so long
will fade. for whatever reason it didn't work out.
while still tender of course you'd ache and upset
and tear and long and wonder why wonder what
thinking you could have done something another
way to make it last. to make it fit. to make it stay.
then one day when you least expect it the sting
the emotions the story of then will be lifted.
it will come as a surprise when you say your past
no longer has hold of you. this is when you know
you have learned and grown. you wish that old
chapter of yours well and just like energy that
lets go and moves on so will you. it will be okay.

***

you are the reminder and the spark. the incredible boost someone needs. they come to you. they come to you. what a beam you are. what a being you are.

the way you walk the weigh you talk there is a different groove. a unique move that wasn't quite there or noticeable back then. you've been through a thing or two that lifts you that lights you that helps you breathe in any condition. you've matured and bloomed. matured and bloomed. and when the aches come again and the tenders come again and the past pasts again you have that walk of you. you have that talk of you. that rises above what hurt you. that rises above what tried to hurt you. that rises above what tries to stop you. nothing and no one can stop you anymore.

starting point.

recognize and remove toxic people out of your life.

you already know this.

soon)whenever soon is or was(the very thing that kept you up will be behind you. you will be unclenched in your body and free in your mind. a previous occupant of your love will be a distant memory. a photo. an old story that has less and less emotional power over you that keeps you from living. you'll wonder what it was about that chapter that made you so fixated on that. you so wanted it and now you don't. time will do that if you fill that time with the active practice of working in yourself. focusing on yourself. when you do that you heal and sometimes can't see it. you'll feel it. you'll be shocked when you free yourself by loving yourself.

you already know this. II

you are rare because everyone else is taken.

***

interesting. isn't it. you can say something and won't be heard. then someone says exactly what you said and the person or the entire room you were speaking to respond as if what was said was so profound. yeah. me too. it happens. but for whatever reason it cuts through differently from another mindset. another experience. if it is in a professional setting don't let that slide. speak up and say nah nah i just said that fyi. personally it can equally be as upsetting but you say profound things all the time. but if you are that person who isn't hearing or taking in what someone says but another person says the exact same thing and you take their advice or it lands differently i need you to check yourself and wonder why. get curious about that. messages come from everywhere and everyone but who are you blocking. who are you stopping. be your full you in every space. no matter the power lines. no matter the social dynamics. aware of how you are in all the spheres you influence. all the spheres you presence. all the spheres that get to breathe the same air as you. and put you on the stand and ask yourself the hard questions. ask yourself just the most important questions. can i be me. all of me. who can't i be here. what part of me is being dismissed here. what mask must i wear here. do i belong here. am i loved here. am i honored here. you know the answers. you know the answers. the most important thing now is what will you do with deliberation. what can you do to ensure you are getting what you need so not to keep leaving parts of you at the door in all the spheres you explore.

the only one in your way is you.

the only one in your way is you. overthinking just tells you that there is so much to consider but never let it stop you from doing. you will never get where you want to be if you keep questioning without knocking without opening without stepping without taking doubts and fears and reservations with you. get out of your way.

don't be the one keeping you away from what is waiting for you.

***

start. that's it. that's the secret. the permission slip. the invitation. the push. the sign. and as you go along you will pick up better ways that make it easier but not unless you start. can't fix what hasn't been created. so that part of you that keeps saying one day or once i or maybe later do it now. close this. make a plan. execute the plan. normal to resist or hesitate or insecure. take all that along and breathe through it and pop champagne or pour water to celebrate as you exceed the dreams you've always dreamed.

the most beautiful goodnight
without saying goodnight.

please don't go. not yet. not yet.
you have been the highlight of my
life today. our conversation awakens
parts of me that have been dormant.
if you have the urge to reach back
at any hour don't hesitate. you are
worth waking up with the sun for.
dawn is named after you. maybe
we fall asleep and do this again.

you are worth waking up with the sun for.

every breath is a chance to heal.

every time you avoid yourself
you lose an opportunity to heal.

and healing doesn't always mean
you are broken and need fixing.

healing is an active process to replenish
what was taken from or released from you
in order to begin again for each new you.

you are what healing looks like in sunlight.

arrest the killers of breonna taylor.

the law in kentucky and in 28 other states make it difficult for police officers to be arrested in situations of shooting and self defense)even if they are the ones doing no knock warrants and murdering private citizens in their own homes. homes officers shouldn't be in. homes citizens have every right to protect(. did you know after breonna taylor's boyfriend shot at whom he thought were intruders and the officers never said they were officers they deployed 20 rounds striking her at least 8 times. did you know in the police incident report it was reported that she had no injuries among other errors. this murder happened five months ago)148 days(and nothing. breonna was 26. black. a woman. an emergency medical technician. friend. sister. daughter. human. who for twenty minutes got no medical attention as she breathed her last breath. her life mattered and the law is keeping those who took her life from being held accountable. louisville do better. change the law. vote to make change don't vote to keep change from happening. we should be ashamed of how much red tape and systems of injustice prove more and more that the system is working how it was built to keep so many down.

for breonna taylor
8.10.20

five do not oaths to chant.

do not leave any part of you behind.
do not shrink yourself for anyone.
do not let them de-prioritize you.
do not forget the reasons you are here.
do not think your work is done.

everyone has something to work on. something to unlearn and undo. no one is immune to bias. check your privilege.

***

you are brilliant. let that sink in.

notice what was in the fire and zipped to the top due to so much pressure. now notice what has been dropped back down because things seem to have cooled off. keep advocating for change and demand real change. not placebo change. real sustainable change. finish that book on anti-racism. watch that documentary on hate. go back to that resource on how not to be a performative ally. pay and bring that diversity practitioner to help hold your organization accountable. keep seeking the arrest of those who murdered breonna taylor. do not let up. you can't let this go. you can no longer unsee. you have to commit. you have to recommit. you have to. you have to. we need each other. to do more of what is right not more of what has been cause of such hardship and chaos and division and hurt. getting someone fired when their duty was to serve and protect sends some shockwaves but not enough. so many good officers all it takes is one bad one to make their reputation tougher. this is bigger than policing. this is recognizing human brutality.

more time

focusing on personal goals.
deepening meaningful relationships.
addressing unhealthy habits.
getting to a higher loving self.

less time

worrying about what others think.
promoting imposter syndrome.
allowing negative energy in.
believing true love doesn't exist.

you are a mystery waiting to be unlocked
by those you bless with a key.

***

if you think you can keep running keep covering keep avoiding yourself you will soon have a rude awakening. do it now while you have control. the worst lessons come when you come too late into your own awareness. the one who really loves you may not wait much longer or you'll miss out on what is in front of you because you're too far away from caring about the impact of your actions. being aware isn't a fad. being aware is a super power high up on people's attraction meter.

*eight mistakes you need
to forgive yourself for.*

staying in a relationship too long.
losing people who never understood you.
letting go of special friendships.
wasted energy on those who didn't deserve you.
family drama out of your control.
places you never got to.
people you couldn't love.
souls you hurt.

you are human. and you do things)done things(
you aren't proud of. grow from your mistakes.

you are sometimes too forgiving to others and so much harder on yourself. forgive yourself for the past by doing all the beautiful things you do in your present.

***

your only mistake. your biggest mistake. was punishing you for decisions and behaviors and pursuits and thoughts and paths you thought best served you at the time. you could only do so much. can only do so much. you are a good heart in hard times. don't measure yourself off of hardship alone. measure yourself on the lessons you have taken with you. grown with you. take care of you better. give yourself some slack. give yourself permission to human and fumble and figure and unlearn so that the next time)there is always a next time(you can choose another choice. you can make up for what was crushing. you should allow yourself to forgive yourself for losing your footing.

let's talk is a love language.
it says:

come to me. listen without reservation.
let there be no misunderstanding between us
that divides us that barriers us that pushes us
away. pour. spill. give. may we breathe with
each other. love on each other. make contact
emotionally with each other. let's share space.
talk space. go where our words need to take us.
you are not in trouble. you are not in trouble.
we just need to catch up. we are behind. gather
your belongings your feelings your uncertainties
your uncried tears and let's break together. rest
together. what do you need from me. i need
this from you. your everything is safe with me.
unguard with me. open here. let's love here.

two notes about growth.

when you grow others might notice.
when you grow others might not notice.

***

they will always notice what you present to them. maybe not in how you want them to receive it or see it see it. no matter in their noticing)or not noticing(should it impact your mood or your next move. then you will know if you did the work only for them or for you. the point of growth)in bettering yourself healing yourself breathing for yourself(is about you. because no one can take that away from you. take note and grow for yourself. and if someone validates a change in you out loud then that is just the universe giving them language to remind you that you may still have some more growing to do. growing never stops.

you are evergrowing. everevergrowing. rooting into places you never thought you would root to. but you are there. you will get there. and sometimes you won't see how you got there. how you grew there. how you could have possibly ended up where you ended up. but that isn't the ending)where you are(there is another end and another end after that. you just have to see each as beginning as more learning as more loving as more possibility and take what you have always taken with you. you. you. evergrowing you.

the you you need to know more of.

i wish you could see the light you are. the depth you are. the sight you are. but magic can't see itself or feel itself. so let me show you. i'll spend my life sharing your glory. your story. your royalty.

don't fake full when feeling empty.

don't fake full when feeling empty.
don't fake full when feeling empty.
don't fake full when feeling empty.
don't fake full when feeling empty.
don't fake full when feeling empty.
don't fake full when feeling empty.
don't fake full when feeling empty.
don't fake full when feeling empty.
don't fake full when feeling empty.
don't fake full when feeling empty.
don't fake full when feeling empty.
don't fake full when feeling empty.
don't fake full when feeling empty.
don't fake full when feeling empty.
don't fake full when feeling empty.
don't fake full when feeling empty.
don't fake full when feeling empty.
don't fake full when feeling empty.
don't fake full when feeling empty.
don't fake full when feeling empty.
don't fake full when feeling empty.
don't fake full when feeling empty.
don't fake full when feeling empty.
don't fake full when feeling empty.
don't fake full when feeling empty.
don't fake full when feeling empty.
don't fake full when feeling empty.
don't fake full when feeling empty.
don't fake full when feeling empty.
don't fake full when feeling empty.
don't fake full when feeling empty.
don't fake full when feeling empty.

four stops to put in place to better appreciate yourself.

stop underestimating yourself.
stop undermining yourself.
stop underwhelming yourself.
stop undervaluing yourself.

***

you get in your head and question what you have to offer. if you are good enough. if you will be chosen. if they will like you. if what you say will be understood. a lot of if's to keep track of and they keep coming. anytime you are in a new environment. anytime you apply for a new position or program or opportunity. and even when you are accepted you think you have to prove yourself. it is a constant warfare against the you that has and always will be top choice. best choice. the choice. only choice. for anyone. for anything. for any any. but it is on you to believe that. it is on you to realize that what you know and who you are and how you are has gotten you this far. that so many)even if you do not know them(talk highly of you and word travels fast. words about you precede you but just because you can't hear it doesn't mean it isn't being said. it is. an infinite amount of more times than you think. trust yourself and stop closing the box in on yourself. there is no box that you fit in. quit putting yourself in one by throwing yourself under when you've always been an over kind of lover. an over kind of heart. an over kind of wonder. better appreciate yourself. better appreciate yourself. stop underestimating yourself. stop undermining yourself. stop underwhelming yourself. stop undervaluing yourself. other people will do that to you. don't do that to you. you are good enough. you will be chosen. you will be liked. you will be what you set your heart on. make sure to set your heart on beautiful truth.

when taken for granted.

it is easy for someone to make plans for you. to speak for you. to use you up for their own advantage that gives their life ease without considering what burdens what stress what labor it inflicts on you. so when you are feeling taken for granted and you want so badly to get out get away get gone get better sometimes you can't see yourself. sometimes you can't feel how tense you are and how short your own fuse gets towards others. towards those closest. towards your own energy. and you carry that everywhere and you make yourself more and more and more and more and more heavy. and you begin to take others for granted. you shift what is being given to you and you give it back. back into spaces you have a bit more control. back into spaces it shouldn't be planted. but everything from you grows. so be mindful not to take soiled goods and seed them next to you. seed them towards the sky. place all that negative into your palms and crush it. look under your nails and get all the dirt it left behind. grind it to its smallest pieces. make it ash. make it unidentifiable. blow it away with your affirmation. with your positive intent. with your perspective. telling it that it isn't yours. that you will not be taken advantage or disadvantage anyone else. this is your control. this is your power. this is your magic. to turn toxic treatment into gold. to let it go. to decide whether or not it is worth your time to say something in word or by action. to set boundaries and stand by them. to take care of you when you feel like no one else is considering you. they think their behavior towards you is okay but when you respectfully push back. when you turn their statement into a question for them to answer. when you give yourself permission to stop holding your feelings hostage to keep others satisfied at your own souls expense. when you breathe and say nah this ain't gonna slide. you can't be taken for granted. you can't be taken advantage of. you can't be pushed over. never again.

what may never come.

an apology.
closure.

fifteen deep breaths to let in.

let in people who earn your trust.
let in love that deserves your heart.
let in kindness that fills your bucket.
let in light to heal your traumas.
let in patience to slow your busy.
let in celebration to honor your grind.
let in affirmations to see yourself.
let in courage to test your purpose.
let in intimacy to caress your soul.
let in forgiveness to let go of your past.
let in imagination to vision your future.
let in vulnerability to wash away your fears.
let in hope to weather your doubts.
let in joy to remember your why.
let in rest to relax refresh rejuvenate you.

you are the deepest deepest breath. the highest highest high. you complete the completed and still have love to spare.

***

rest should be your theme. your mantra. your reminder. you shouldn't just rest once and call it done. rest is an active choice to stop. to stop. to stop. and slow. and slow. and slow. no matter if those around you are in a rush a frenzy a bind a deadline a jam. even then there are breaths that need to be taken. don't forget to breathe. breathe now if you haven't all day. sit. close. inhale. exhale. in. out. again. again. no one should ever take your rest away. if they try then get a far distance from them.

two truths about pain.

pain makes us human and pain selfishly fuels our intense desire to love what makes us suffer.

you deserve this.

to heal.

everyone deserves healing.

four truths that have always been true.

your feelings are valid.
you deserve deep requited bountiful love.
your heart is a beautiful garden.
you bloom when you choose to be yourself.

people will try to knock you down to outwit
and prove they know more than you do about
you and your life. do not engage. breathe them
in peace. maintain your peace. and carry your
truths with you in the other direction unbothered.

***

there shouldn't have to be reminders to be yourself. to be able to go where your heart feels free. but this place and some people that feel overcome with this notion to barrier and displace others make it so that there has to be outcries to live peacefully while they want to keep their lives to themselves which only further encages them and their unhappiness. push back. they never had the key to your heart. they made it up. break free from the framework and system that keeps you in a box that comforts them and deny yourself from ever going back. care for your life and less about who says you can't what your soul can. have the audacity to bloom and bloom and bloom and bloom. have the audacity to not blocade your heart to them. have the audacity to keep open the hope that they will get out of their own way out of their own cage and into what blooms them. for that is the peace withheld from them. and you are better than that. your heart is a beautiful garden that inspires so many other beautiful gardens to be just that. wild. gentle. free. welcoming. anything less than wouldn't be you. be you. dear garden. be you.

twelve songs written in the key of you.

can't get enough of you. your love is ooh.
tongue tied when you are on my mind. chasing
you will be the greatest adventure of a lifetime.
hearts forget to beat when you speak. night
get here quick so i can see the stars envy
your light. the water in you quenches
fills and heals. you don't even know
how beautiful you are. blessing.
amazing grace. favorite lyric.
you make every day sweet.

***

did you sing that. did you hymn that. did you breathe that. i hope you did. i hope you slowly went back to each line and underlined you. i hope you wrote more lines next to the ones unwritten unspoken and wrote twelve more. where did you stop. why did you stop. which took your breath. which helped your heart beat faster. which lyric made you melt. someone is singing this this moment. someone saved this page and wrote your name and scratched out *you* to be more specific. and right now you don't believe that right now you think this is about another person. nope. this is about you. the melody of you. the harmony of you. the key of you. the stars you can't even see are twinkling to your rhythm. you can hear them if you felt your body go warmer. you can feel them if you felt your skin begin to tingle. i hope these songs are on your playlist. i hope you replay them a thousand times each. i hope when you return to this note you'll feel the same as you did the first time you fell healthy in love. the first time you told your person they were your person and the rush it was when they told you you were their first.

three reminders to ease your mind.

when you give yourself what you need
no one has the power to take it away.

when you give yourself what you want
no one has the power to take it away.

when you give yourself what you deserve
no one has the power to take it away.

any extra from others allows you to spill all over.

***

what a spilling you are. what a blessing you are. when you open the way you open there is possibility that wasn't possible before. when you love the way you love there is a calm that fills voids. pages have been written about you and the surface has yet to be scratched. so much more to find. so much more to admire. it is your give it is your love it is your xo that is mystery. that is searched for. that is longed for. that is buried treasure. buried treasure in mind. buried treasure in heart. buried treasure in soul. each dimension of you spills effortlessly into another and another and another and another. some want diamonds and some want riches and some want laughter and some want peace and some want truth and some want degrees and some want articles posted about them to show their success their worth their validity. your worth is somewhere in-between. your worth is internal. an eternal inning. learning more of love and self worth and meaning and belonging. that is richness. that is you. there can be all of those things when connected to your purpose. when connected to your why. your wealth is you.

five signs you're going in circles.

same outcome happens.
nothing different changes.
you keep getting hurt.
no one ever apologizes.
unable to get closure.

you are at a breaking point beyond being fed up. old moves feel like you're frozen in time. playing reels in your head knowing how it ends because you've experienced the scene. this go round choose another route. another exit strategy. reclaim a new beginning. close the loop or continue spinning with the wrong person.

***

no matter how hard it is you have to choose to do something different. to choose what you typically choose to flee from. to choose to let go instead of hold on. to choose to finish instead of drag on. to choose to examine instead of pretending it isn't there. to choose to head on to choose to try on to choose to lean in to choose to this time. holding off for a time that feels right is just putting off to then put off again. the bracing and the stressing and the pitting before the interaction is what is distracting you from facing you. but when you do it)whatever needs to be done and faced(you will tell yourself there was nothing for you to have been fearful of in the first place. there is lesson in that tension. don't let it handcuff you from the next challenge. at first glance everything looks terrifying when it's unknown but that doesn't mean shy away or condemn or villify. it means breathe into the unknown with curiosity to learn something you haven't learned yet about yourself. even if it's hard.

re-introduce yourself.

you've always been a vibe. always. now more people are being introduced to your kind of love language.

***five ways to say no
without saying no.***

i'm unavailable at the moment. take care.
now isn't a good time. i appreciate the ask.
unfortunately i cannot accept. be well.
i have to pass. thanks for thinking of me.
perhaps next season. when things clear up.

it's okay if you are not interested or don't have
the energy or want to be left alone. advances
or asks or invitations are in your corner to accept
or decline without the added pressure of others.
you can be respectful in your decline. sometimes
you have to be clear to make no room for doubt.
it's okay if you have other priorities you must
focus on. you have a right to pass and say no.

***

society. people. systems. all put pressure on us to feel bad for saying no. to have to do things to please others and not make them uncomfortable. release yourself from that expectation. say no more often. of course be kind and respectful but let them know with a no nah i'm good in your own special language. and if you are that person too stubborn to take no or hear no you have a lot a lot a lot a lot a lot of work to do. check yourself. no one needs that added weight that added load that added heaviness on top of what is already being labored. the best thing that can ever be done is to add in your ask that *if it's too much it's all good either way is fine.* you'd be surprised just how adding a simple phrase like that fosters deep breaths of relief that people truly appreciate and remember.

rest is a love language.
it says:

take a break. take a breath. prioritize you
and do not apologize for choosing you. it is
long overdue and you deserve all the time to
get your balance. get your reward for being.
resist the urge to announce to declare to share
your plan to retreat. just retreat. relax. lay. go.
do. whatever brings you joy. brings you peace.
tell your body tell your mind tell your soul
everything it needs to hear. needs to feel. fill
you up with all the things you have been missing.
no one gives this to you. you give ease to you.
pause for you. notice what is most important.
and while away you'll know what you need
to do upon return. thank you for going slow.

***

rest looks good on you. refreshes you. replenishes you. restarts you. sometimes it seems too far. too distant. too unavailable. but reach for it. plan for it. demand for it. it is your right to recharge. your right to respond to your body to your mind to your soul. go there. to that place that fills you. and keep going there. you deserve to slow down after all that traveling you have been doing. all that stress you've been carrying. all that stuff you've been planning. all that trying to keep everything from falling. rest dear heart. rest dear heart. and do this on the daily even if you say there is no time to daily. make it happen. make you happen. make you daily. routine you daily. start with sixty seconds at a minimum to prove you can carve out time. to whisper or to quiet whatever clears your mind.

when you want something real.

when you want something real
but you keep but you keep but
you keep settling for the same
for the same for the same the
exact replica of what was of
what was of what was of w-
hat was means you aren't
ready aren't ready aren't
ready to let go to let go
to let go to let go.

when you want something real but you keep settling for the same exact replica of what was means you aren't ready to let go.

***

when do you know you are ready. how do you know you aren't letting go. when do you know that what you have isn't real. how do you know you are settling. important questions to unpack and consider and explore to see where each one takes you. where each one thorns you. where each one pushes you. to wonder more. to why more. to go as far deep into the unknowing as you are capable and keep going. this is only if you want to search for patterns. this is only if you are willing to be aware of the ripples you make. this is only if you are ready)if you want to know if you are ready(for something different. for someone different. to re-surface from this search. if the goal is to do this temporarily to impress outside of you nothing will transpire. nothing will last. nothing will change. letting go looks like you having as many of your answers from your journey and choosing to accept what they revealed and moving on.

what love isn't.

cruel.
punishing.
vindictive.
withholding.

if you cannot be yourself and fear rejection
from the one closest to you that isn't safe love.
that is harsh and not the beautiful language
you deserve. love is a difficult dance but once
you find the beat and the rhythm of one another
you'll never be empty. always full. always full.

***

trust what energy tells you. follow where the invisible language takes you. listen. you can't go wrong when you're in tune to your soul. and if someone keeps trying to give you what isn't in your frequency. isn't in your vocabulary. isn't in your needs. then they will never experience the full full full of you. only a partial you because they can't seem to understand the heart of you. and that is devastating to only experience some of you. so do not accept. do not allow. do not wait. you know how to speak their language. you can't continue having one-sided conversations when you speak multiple languages at home. you can't keep shortening your words and shortening your emotions and shortening your being to comfort their shortcomings. to comfort their selfish. to comfort their language. it has to be level. it has to be fair. it has to be mutual. it has to be both and. they can't play keep away with your heart and not expect for you to catch on. that isn't love. that is game. and love isn't about winning. love is a field of dreams you to get to awake in.

we need each other.

one day you'll realize hate wasn't worth it. that we all wanted the same things. but too many are unwilling to see or hear or care enough to be kind or interested in what makes us who we are. maybe take some of that bravery and talk to someone who has a different background or experience or perspective than you. you don't learn when all you absorb is what confirms your own biases. we need each other before it is too late.

what does this have to do with love language. and why is it in this book. why is this filtered on these pages instead of on its own. this is why. this is because. we so badly want to rush away and ignore reality. to distract ourselves and hope someone else out there figures this stuff out. but all of this is connected. all of this is the same. we all have blindspots and we all have areas to negotiate. but we can't wait for a higher up or a traumatic event or a book club or a forced professional development or an open space conversation to dive in. to be too late. so this could be a start or a continuation or a pause. if you have read this far this serves as another invitation to probe into you more. to take this to task and wonder. just wonder. and why. just why. and lean on someone you trust to be your accountability. to be your thought partner. to be your mirror. to soundboard. to springboard. to loveboard. and perhaps they will join. perhaps they will read. perhaps they will unlearn. but this is about you. do your work. lead yourself to undo your own stuff. the hard stuff you ignore. the hard stuff no one really gave air time to. the hard stuff that makes you uncomfortable just thinking about it. you can break that discomfort by breathing into it. by being into it. by being into you. the hard stuff can be fun stuff if you introduce it differently. if you let go of thinking it is supposed to make you feel guilt or shame or fragile. you'll see that it's all about helping you be a better human.

twelve positive assumptions.

assume positive intent.
assume people are trying their best.
assume people will keep their word.
assume problems can be resolved.
assume today will be better than yesterday.
assume someone looks up to you.
assume you have more love to give.
assume giving is your soul purpose.
assume change starts with you.
assume grass isn't greener on the other side.
assume black lives matter.
assume all lives matter.

***

they may take your kindness for weakness. or your smile as passive. or your quiet as complicit. but they need to understand you give more benefits or more chances and more opportunity to begin again. you do this for yourself as well. but when they intentionally take and take and take and give nothing. or aren't around until they need something it's time to re-evaluate. sometimes people need to be told about themselves even if it's hard to hear.

patience is a love language.
it says:

don't rush. don't force. don't get in the way.
trust that what is for you won't miss you won't
skip you won't ignore you. timing is everything.
the answer the fate the feeling the prize is
headed towards you while you pace towards it.
accept. accept. accept. embrace. embrace.
embrace. no need to anger or upset or sad. have
faith. prepare and continue and give and move
and tool your strength. you are being polished.
sharpened. blossoming. ready and not knowing
how ready you already are. pay attention. soon
)sooner than you think(the horizon will breach
your shore because you are shore and horizon.
wait without suffering and become whole. full.

many nights and days have zoomed by and some good some bad some still pricking you. and what you feel has been formed against you still hasn't prevailed because it is you. the faith you have in you is so strong. so tight. so bound in believing better it sometimes loses its battle to thorns. voices and energies and dramas of others. you're human growing through. growing up. growing down. growing everywhere even if new growth isn't overt. patience, dear heart. you are you and those are the best hands to be in. you are you and that is beyond enough to be. so confirm this. so adorn this. don this to your heart on your skin on something to repeat when you are in disbelief. because time will tell of your sojourn. time will tell of your pleas. it can be hard to want something so bad you don't want to wait for it you want it now but when you get it when it isn't ready you will wait even longer. so keep doing. what you need is coming.

love is a language understood without words.

love is a language understood without words.

a beautiful libation
to pour for yourself.

it's okay if you aren't perfect.
it's okay if you forgot something.
it's okay if you ran out of time.
it's okay if you didn't make sense.

grace. dear heart. grace. give yourself
a break. a pass)a multitude of passes(.
to fumble. to fail. to mistake. to miss.
to live. to live. to live. you hold so much.
high so much. that your own standards
can be difficult to exceed. no one notices
because even your low or your flaws and
errors are beautiful. masterful.

water crashes. you can crash, too. and still be incredible.

***

quit being so hard on yourself. everything you do is always high caliber and meaningful and inspiring. your "off" is still amazing. because it's you. shake it off and remember no one probably even noticed. you kept going and that is what truly matters. chin up. heart up.

enough is a love language.
it says:

i'm torn. i'm tired. i've had it up to here. clearly it doesn't register that my life matters. that my body is target. practice. a means to end. get off. get away. why don't you hear me. see me. stop. maybe take a breath. maybe you need to do something else. this is not your calling. to take what isn't yours to take is inhumane. indecent. uncalled for. terrorism. abysmal. this rage bottled up isn't because i've told you once. or twice. or three times. or one hundred. but thousands. millions. what will it cost to finally get through. you don't want to be a hashtag or need a movement. why do you think i do. this is the final warning. final call. this is too much.

it is one thing to learn about racism. it's another to experience racism. to see yourself in the news over and over and over like it's nothing. like it's normal. like it's business as usual. it's one thing to raise funds to support a cause and another to be the cause. to be in and not looking in. the trauma it causes inside to be another casualty that looks like you. like your father. like your mother. like your son. like your daughter. like your brother. like your kin. if you really cared once would be enough. if you really cared it wouldn't happen twice. if you really cared you would shut the world down. if you really cared. justice for all black lives. we need security. this is why the black panthers existed. why self defense classes became mandatory. sadly this isn't new and another hashtag will be upon us soon. healing prayers for jacob blake and his family. please recover. please recover.

for jacob blake
8.24.20

an anti-racist statement.

if anti-racism isn't part
of your healing you aren't
really healing.

no one is immune to racism. it is a toxin in the air. you breathe it in. daily. constantly. particles are in you and you don't even know it. impacts how you treat people. see people. love people. avoid people. racism is a symptom of something so much more sinister. it operates without someone needing to pull strings. it is in the bloodstream. passed down generation after generation. if you really are about healing and growing and making this place better you need to focus on pulling racism out of you. then be like harriet tubman and go back and help others. if you call yourself a healer or in a healing profession and do not include anti-racism in your practice you can't call yourself a holistic healer. if you are a leader of an organization and do not have anti-racism in your strategic plan you aren't really a safe space. if you are someone who says i don't see color or i have one black friend you will never truly heal. everyone is impacted. everyone. what you shrug off is an actual crisis. a slow genocide. nothing civil about this war.

definitions of privilege
that are sadly unknown.

the ability to overlook deny dismiss and intentionally ignore someone else's lived experience while choosing not to recognize one's own advantages that shelters them and prevents them from witnessing bias unfairness and violations to life and liberty; to be free from blame or ridicule by being idle in the complicit acts of overt injustice; the option to turn away from turn off turn down issues that do not look like or sound like or feel like problems they directly or indirectly benefit from by simply rejecting its very existence.

***

what is it like to go years)plural even decades(without being caged. by being able to walk into a church into a protest into a school into a movie theatre and take lives and walk away with your life and a full stomach. i really want to know what blinders feel like to not be able to see even if you stared right at it that gives you no pause no fast heartbeat no knots to unknot to do nothing or say nothing while volcanoes erupt around you. must be nice to live toll free. to live unaware behind i didn't know and that must have been awful i'm sorry to hear that happened to you. we all have privileges but yours hit different and you know it but just can't admit it or else you would have to live up to the ridicule of those keeping hold of your secret. get from behind that privilege curtain and be a real human. if you fear losing likes and love for standing up for what is right while real lives are being lost. taken. like its nothing. you need to check yourself. wrong is wrong. check your privilege.

if reading this made you feel uncomfortable and you want to stop. take a breath. lean in. this is important. keep going. you are loved.

five types of rest you deserve.

mental rest. quiet the mind. reduce the noise.
emotional rest. moments to feel and unfeel.
spiritual rest. find inner peace. deep. slow peace.
physical rest. lay down. relax. body breaths.
social rest. retreat from people. places. stress.

no need to explain yourself. your feelings.
your wants. your needs. go get what you deserve.
you shouldn't hesitate when it comes to you.
release all that pressure that doesn't belong.

***

rest is for everyone. not just for some. some people feel like it is a privilege and not a right. sadness in that statement. to keep people away from their own health. their own sanity. you are not a workhorse. you are a lightworker. a special being who needs time to rest not work yourself til you are nothing left. life isn't about working it is about loving. too bad we have been convinced to work five days a week to live and only two to love. change that. change you. push back against work-life balance and turn it into life-work balance into love-life balance. we all have to make ends meet. to afford to roof. to afford to eat. to afford to exist. but it shouldn't consume all our time. it shouldn't consume our heart and sap us to just want to not be bothered by the ones we really want to be around. so rest is a start. to say yes more to self. to say no more to the stuff that gets in the way. and that be okay. that be the to-do. to go down the long list and decide what to remove and what to approve. practice putting you on there. to top three you. to say for every time i center me i grant me more occasions to love me.

you already know this. III

you are an awe. a tincture. a medicine. a healing.
that too often is forgotten. too often left unnoticed.
but how impossible it is not to see you. not to seek
you. not to wish the weight of you was anywhere else
but here but here but here but here but here
where you are abundantly loved. when you find yourself
in spaces people forget who you are
do not go out of your way to remind them.
soon enough they will awaken from their
slumber and you will be where you have
always been. serving and caring and
working and inspiring and loving
the way only you love. deeply.
let your light speak for itself.

***

to those who get to meet you. get to feel you. get to see you. in person. in flesh. on screen. who get to know you know you)not the digital you(i say they are the recipients of finding the last arc. the last treasure. the last last. the most beautiful find. a rare rare. and if someone loses you they will spend the rest of their life searching for a soul like yours. what an honor you are. what an honor you are. don't you get that. don't you see that. don't you see you. sometimes you can't. and that's okay. but the special in you is too vibrant not to set in front of you. too magnetic not to attract you. too chilly not to wrap you. these words don't hold a candle to the heat you bring. to the heat you are. to the heat you temperature in others. but that is that heart in you. to wander like everyone else. not aboving anyone else. full of beautiful beautiful humility. but you already know this.

flags that let you know
who people really are.

green flags. courteous. loving. supportive. present.
yellow flags. distant. unclear. neutral. unpredictable.
red flags. hurtful. avoidant. disrespectful. uncaring.

you know who someone really is over time but can't always hope they match up to idealistic standards. people are people with their own programming. once they show you them believe them and take mental notes. you deserve golden relationships not fools gold situationships. it is fall. time to pull weeds.

***

it is fall. it is always fall. time to pull weeds. you know who that is. what that means. what to let go. so do it. no more holding back. no more being taken advantage of. no more toxic in your system. no more hoping it will get better. by now you know. by now you've known. and the only thing you can change is you. how you show up. how you freely. how you give. how you love. how you respond. how you grant. and whether you do something quickly or overt or covert or behind the best thing you can do is take care of you. to take you back quickly. overtly. promptly. nowly. heartly. strongly. so you can get to what is most important. so you can see other flags you never thought existed. to breathe healthy air. to be your healthy heir. to dust off your crown and reclaim your throne. time to delay isn't an option. time to change habits that need to be disposed of. so when you pull what you pull you will naturally have the urge to put back. but what you pull should be put out far far from you.

it's okay. IV

it's okay if you just sat for hours and felt unproductive. it's okay if you wanted to fill in the gaps but had nothing left in the tank to give. it's okay if you didn't have energy to battle someone's unkind remark. it's okay if you didn't respond to all those unread messages. i just want you to know it's okay if you need a break and already took a break and break again break now if you haven't. break now if you haven't. it's okay. it's okay. okay.

***what you need to hear but
haven't told yourself yet.***

look how far you've come. there is still some ways to go
)and many ways after that(. and you didn't stop. you didn't quit.
you're still standing. perseverance looks good on you. too many
told you otherwise and didn't believe and doubted or didn't take
you serious but you took you serious. you lated and earlied and
battled and sored and crunched and withstood. you withstood.
lay out all you have done that once felt like a maze and now a well
lit path. every step isn't granted but you make them count. if you're
emotional you should be. all you have manifested. all you had to
give up to find you. those around you are better because of you.
smell your roses love.

***

tell yourself what you need to hear tonight. tell yourself what you
need to feel tonight. give yourself flowers not for ego but for spirit.
for heart. for you. like i don't really think you understand the
magnitude of all the things you have done to get where you are.
how hard it has been but you haven't had the time or taken the
time or didn't think it was worth appreciating you. nah. appreciate
you. you are a big deal. you've been making moves. making waves.
experiencing your own magic sometimes softens the immenseness
it really is. that you really are. so start by laying out every milestone.
every defining moment. every box you have checked. and feel the
awe of your nature. the grand of your mountain. the beauty of your
horizon. my god you do the impossible and do it every single day.
you are unbelievable. unbelievable. smell your roses love. smell
your roses love.

six strengths no one has the power
to ever take away from you. ever.

to feel.
to learn.
to think.
to ask.
to wonder.
to love.

your mind your heart your being is majestic.
what you do and how you love can never be
used against you. may you find peace in who
you are and always remember: you are magic.

***

no one can take away those strengths of yours. the ones they deem soft. the ones they deem unuseful. the ones they deem weak. the ones they deem uncontrollable. the ones they deem unnecessary. the ones they deem too hard for them so they write laws and barrier and criminalize and punish and ignore and elevate ones that suit them. that comfort them. that access them. that power them. but all they are doing is building more walls within themselves. don't worry about what they are doing. get free. stay free. be free.

four signs you still have more healing to do.

still tender.
still hurt.
still denying.
still triggered.

love from you is what will get you through.
will get you to piece back. will get you to trust
your heart again. to love fully instead of partially.
and you have work to do to get there. it's okay
to admit you are protecting yourself. take your time.

***

do not rush yourself to be okay. to skip the grieving. to bypass your feelings. just because the world is opening up a bit more and going back to normal)it never was normal(that doesn't mean go back to running away from yourself. go towards yourself. be with yourself and pinpoint the roots that need new water and the branches that need cutting. take your time with yourself. embrace yourself. don't ignore you the way you ignored you before. lean into you. continue working on you. centering you. honoring you. by doing the things that motivated you that inspired you that ignited you. don't lose the momentum. stay in your moment. this moment right now. lock in and make anew. set new goals and love towards them. rock them. surpass them. not so you can say you did it but because you can be proud of you. for not forgetting you. for not putting a bookmark in that part of your chapter and moving on without finishing and tending and ellipsissing you. don't do that to you. don't go unattended. unwatered. keep watering. keep watering. there is more healing to do. more growing to do. more loving to do.

ten necessities to pick up.

pick up exercising. take care of your body.
pick up listening. hear what is being said.
pick up questioning. always ask why.
pick up awarenessing. get to know you better.
pick up following. your heart needs attention.
pick up intimacy. romance yourself.
pick up advocacy. fight for what is right.
pick up language. learn what isn't being said.
pick up friendships. check on your people.
pick up yourself. love the soul you're becoming.

***

raise this glass for you. pour one if you don't have one. raise it high. above your heart. to your heart. close your eyes and repeat: i'm getting through because i am me and me isn't perfect but me is enough. me is proof. me is proud even when no one says they are proud of me. now say it again like you mean it. only this time throw in some words you've been meaning to tell yourself. then pick up where you left off. don't sell yourself short by getting to you last.

return to love.

no matter how many lovers you try to fill that emptiness with they will fall into the depths of your dependence.

return to love. not in someone else.
but in yourself.

four masks to stop wearing.

the mask that doesn't take responsibility.
the mask that shuts off how you truly feel.
the mask that covers who you really are.
the mask that makes others comfortable.

may the mask you sometimes wear protect you.
keep certain energies off of you. shield you from
people who don't have good intentions. but do
not wear them so it prevents you from being you.
don't forget who you are.

***

if you have to pretend to be someone you aren't around your people then those aren't your people. and if they pretended to know you they lost you and whoever lost you never knew what they had. and that's okay. you gave your all. and you will give again. love again. try again. don't look for fault in you. you did nothing wrong. and nothing to fix or affix or fixate on. something someone somewhere better is bound for you. on to you. coming your way. already there. moments closing in on your expectations. aboving your dreams. answering your manifestations and all your prayers. only this time it will last love.

it's unfair that so many just don't know what to do when they come across one such as you. you can lead someone to your water but can't force them to love you the way you need to be loved. the one the one the one for you won't need to be led or convinced. your one will meet you where you are and show you a love that rocks your world and gives you the butterflies you've been giving yourself.

8 lessons

you do not need to ride the same wave as others.
you do not need to shorten your name.
you do not need to be a two line quotation.
you do not need to break yourself to be accepted.
you will find your voice. you will find your why.
you will find your way. you will find your place.

no matter how unclear your path you are still on
your path. you will get to where you get to if you
focus on your how to. your got to. just follow you.

***

you will get stuck into the what people are doing. the fads that are popping. the trends that get follows. the aesthetic that buzzes. but all that becomes dust. all that is mirage. all that won't last. but you will emerge if you get out of the crowd. if you get back on your path. if you trust in your story. if you emulate yourself. where you're supposed to be may not be clear now but it will be clearer. revealed when you believe in you. true to you. be fully you. and when you do that. when you carve out your own path and vision for your own you sometimes will find yourself alone. not in support. but in craft. not in feeling. but in industry. because you are blazing. a blaze. amazing. can you hear the crash of you. can you hear the tones of you. can you hear the magic of you. all the lessons in you. all the waves of you. all the ways of you. leading. guiding. showing. forming. homing. what doesn't even exist yet. not everyone is interested in the unexplored they go towards what is known. you are called to the wild. to seek and bring back what you find. so in your next chapter peace be your wild. peace be your beautiful wild.

ten apologies you don't need to give.

don't apologize for your resting.
don't apologize for your spacing.
don't apologize for your retreating.
don't apologize for your breathing.
don't apologize for your slowing.
don't apologize for your ignoring.
don't apologize for your snoozing.
don't apologize for your awaying.
don't apologize for your retiring.
don't apologize for your inning.

don't ask for permission to grant yourself rest. don't ask for permission to get some time. don't ask permission to bring you back to you. too much going on that permissions have gone out the window. the only permission you need is from yourself. the world will keep turning but not the same with you out here fuming. rest. it isn't a soon to do. it is a now to do. turn your phone off. don't answer emails. don't wonder what other people are doing. take care of your home. get your house in order. order everything you need and do that more often. and tell your no resting people to rest with you. hiatus as long as you need. don't make an announcement just do it. and when you come back)if you decide to(we will rejoice. if you do not come back we will know you are doing what is best for you and rejoice(. and if this is the last page you get to that prompted your rest. good. no need to go further. this will be yet another invitation to step away from. to disconnect. to deactivate. to not even away message but to let being away be the message itself. i hope you get away. i hope you rehabilitate your soul your light your energy. soon. seconds before you turn this page to the next. if this is part of your rest that is a blessing. turn into your rest. turn into your rest. rest.

*four be's to remind you
to be gentle with yourself.*

be good enough for you.
be gracious to your heart.
be cautious of what you say.
be content with who you are.

there you are
all of who you are
others might turn away
but never turn away
from you.

***

it can be hard being around people who have nothing but good happening to them. happiness can repel you if you aren't feeling positive. try not to let their happiness be your comparison. be happy for them. root for them. and dig deep into your being to check in on your needs. any voids that need attention. can't be on all the time but if you are off don't force yourself into someone else's light pretending to be okay. your wellbeing is important. first step. ask yourself how you are doing. how are you really doing. and if you don't want to talk to someone skip to step three and write how you are feeling down. if you did step two of sharing with someone out loud then hit up step four which is to do it all again. be gentle with yourself. you hear this now more and more. you have scoffed and ignored and pushed that phrase down. what does it mean. what can it really mean. you decide. perhaps at its core it is guiding words from yourself to yourself. if you don't like the phrase create your own reminder your own mantra to be. write that down. say it now.

something beautiful you haven't felt
that you really need to feel right now.

where are you from because you aren't like most.
not of this place. like you have been here before and know
something no one else here knows. as if you know the secret. are
the secret. staring at you is like witnessing the world being created
and re-created over and over again. how are you.
how are you so unique. how are you so rare. how
are you gracing us when we don't deserve to
breathe your air. you. oh heartbeat. are.
you. oh. giver. are. you. oh lover. are.
effortlessly everything. any attempt to duplicate
the light of you the way you light up a room isn't
possible. isn't replicable. you are once in a life
time. once in a honey moon. you are refreshing.

***

what is it that you need right now. what is it that you need to feel right now. take the time to think about that now. this isn't just any book. this isn't just any check the box got through the pages what's next. this is you. part of you. experience you. alone in you with these words and your heart and you. do you have what you need. did you margin them here or somewhere nearby. maybe you circled somewhere and highlighted somewhere and got what you needed already. do you still need that. what you need changes. who you are changes. but who you are to you should always remain constant. being there constant. being here constant. slowing here constant. holding here constant. because what is true about you isn't true about others because no one can be you. who are you. where are you. questions only you can deeply answer how you would answer.

losing is a beautiful happening.

maybe one day means today. when you realize that person you are reaching for just isn't going to reach back the way you want. the way you need. the way you hope. and that is hard. that is heart hurting to accept. because the waiting has consumed so much of you that letting go feels like losing you. losing time invested. losing)if you think about it(is a beautiful happening. losing tells you more about you than getting what you want. it tells you what you don't need. and you don't need someone unwilling to meet you in the deep end of your love. move on. move. on.

fall. fall. fall.

when you fall tell them you aren't down.
when you fall tell them you are resting.
when you fall tell them you are cool.
when you fall tell them nothing.

may this season recover you. wrap you how you
want to and need to be held. may every challenge
reveal its lesson and grow you. in the slowing
in the quiet in the change may you find comfort.
protect your heart. learn balance and seek wonder.

***

when you fall you grow in places the light couldn't get to. remember this is your season. lean into it. grow into it. find peace and then winter in it. stay there and learn there. decompress there. you'll bloom because you're already blooming but you'll bloom some more. you'll spring with added color and remind you of where you fell before. where you've fallen. when your fall before last prepared you for what was to come. what does fall mean to you. what does fall mean to you. do you see it as strength or do you see it as weakness. is there a primary feeling when you think of falling. did a recent fall come to heart. where is your mind taking you this instant. bring your attention back to this last refrain. when you fall tell them you aren't down. when you fall tell them you are resting. when you fall tell them you are cool. when you fall tell them nothing. fall. fall. fall. when you fall look for the lesson that is waiting for your looking. when you fall look for the you that's been waiting for your looking.

choose yourself.

today. choose yourself. today. choose yourself a bit more. love you a bit more. someone will say something unkind and you will hold it like truth. don't grab onto it. let it pass. words from the past clutch you from moving how you want to move. but today. today kick them to the curb. do what was told of you not to do not to wear not to enjoy not to pursue. just do. live and love and go be. choose yourself right now. even if today is the only day. then do it again tomorrow. and the next. and the next. and the next. until it becomes ritual. be your ritual. be your beautiful.

choose yourself. this isn't selfish. although they would want you to think that. want you to feel that. want you to sacrifice yourself for the sake of them.

choosing yourself looks like

working on your shadows. putting your wellness first. no more self-abandonment. saying no to the things that drain you. no longer shrinking to make others more comfortable. not betraying yourself seeking the approval of others. setting and maintaining boundaries. living your truth. choosing to love and accept yourself in your current form. not feeling guilty for the things people try to make you feel guilty for. resting. noticing when you are terrible to yourself for being terrible at choosing yourself. paying attention to the things that make you feel alive and aligned. taking time to discover who you are outside of your day job. listening to your body. doing what brings you joy. finding peace in your alone. breaking from relationships that never or no longer fulfill or serve you. not settling. being assertive. allowing how you truly feel take up space to say what's real. starting over when starting over is the scariest thing to do.

trust yourself.

and so here you are. at a tipping point. in-between. a heart marker. a mind marker. feeling whatever it is you are feeling and thinking whatever it is you are thinking. holding internal motions. finding yourself blocking internal dialogue to decide what must be decided. opinions and expectations and pressures and pressures and pressures press you expect you opine you to those of others. of other. of not you. oh you. oh you. are you. grasp that. firm that. contract that. declare that. you've been here before. you've pro conned and listed and bullet pointed and compared and contrasted and did what you did to do what you had to do. some you agreed and some you againsted. some you went along to keep up with what shouldn't have been kept. let that be that. but this is this. a now. an unknown that is terrifying because there are no steps after it. no seen through it. no net under it. no blueprint or guidebook or roadmap just you and a compass. just you to say the final word. just you to wade in what you have always said you wanted. what you have been playing out since always. what you lose track about in imagination in journal excerpts in heart races. block out everyone else. block out the naysayers. block out the yaysayers. block out everyone who isn't you. see you. do you see you. close your eyes if you have to. can you see you now. can you feel you now. let you be your first responder. come to your aid and answer. believe in you. take that worry with you. you will be successful no matter what. take that fear with you. you will unlock what has always been yours. take that trepidation with you. you will come out on the other side. take that heart with you. you will inspire you each and every time. take that wave with you. you will water and grow all that you plant. take that tenacity with you. you will need all your beautiful tenacity. take that love with you. you will create compassion all around you. trust yourself. trust yourself. trust yourself. trust yourself.

i hope you find resolve in you. even if only a little. i hope your heart opens up a bit wider. even if only a little. i hope you practice something different. even if only a little. i hope you feel loved for the beautiful lover that you are. in the greatest sense of love. in the greatest sense of love. thank you for being you. *xo. adrian michael*

i appreciate you ♥